WHATEVER GETS YOU THROUGH

EDITED BY

STACEY MAY FOWLES
& JEN SOOKFONG LEE

Foreword by JESSICA VALENTI

WHATEVER GETS YOU THROUGH

Twelve Survivors on Life after Sexual Assault

GREYSTONE BOOKS
Vancouver/Berkeley

Greystone Books Ltd.
greystonebooks.com

Cataloguing data available from Library and Archives Canada
ISBN 978-1-77164-373-3 (pbk.)
ISBN 978-1-77164-374-0 (epub)

Copy editing by Shirarose Wilensky
Cover design by Briana Garelli
Text design by Nayeli Jimenez
Proofreading by Jennifer Stewart
Printed and bound in Canada on ancient-forest-friendly paper by Friesens

Excerpt from "I Am Draped in Heavenly Skin" by Joshua Jennifer
Espinoza used with permission of the author.

Greystone Books gratefully acknowledges the Musqueam, Squamish,
and Tsleil-Waututh peoples on whose land our office is located.

Greystone Books thanks the Canada Council for the Arts, the British
Columbia Arts Council, the Province of British Columbia through
the Book Publishing Tax Credit, and the Government of Canada for
supporting our publishing activities.

Canadä

BRITISH COLUMBIA | BRITISH COLUMBIA ARTS COUNCIL
An agency of the Province of British Columbia

Canada Council   Conseil des arts
for the Arts   du Canada

To those who survived in whatever way they could.
To those who keep surviving every day.
To those who are still searching for a way to survive.

CONTENTS

FOREWORD

·

Jessica Valenti

•

I T'S HARD TO be in this moment, yet again: a moment when the culture seems to have caught up to what feminists have been saying all along—that things are bad, worse than you think. Because all of a sudden you have hope—hope that things can get better, hope that maybe we've finally hit the tipping point on people believing women and all survivors of sexual assault.

But we know better. Those of us who write about feminism, or think about these issues, or walk through the world female know that no matter how many people come forward there is an unmovable fact: men believe other men, and they disbelieve survivors. No matter how many contrite apologies are issued by men who have been caught with their pants down, sometimes literally, they are continually given the benefit of the doubt. What does that leave us with?

In my worst moments, I think it leaves us with nothing—that we're back where we started. In a time when abusers are outed every week and survivors are still blamed, it's easy to feel as if we've made no progress at all. But that's not the truth. What we have—what we've always had, and what we have today more than ever—is our voices. Our stories. The lives we live in spite of it all.

Our ability to continue to tell our stories in the face of disbelief and hatred is an incredible, powerful, *hopeful* thing. Because although sharing these experiences—whether in books, in a hashtag, or just in conversation—is in part an act of solidarity, it's also done with a glimmer of belief that things can be better.

After all, they can't call all of us liars.

They can't continue to say that it's not that bad, or that the statistics around harassment or rape are overblown. The more of us who speak and take up space, the less believable *they* become.

And that's how we win. We overwhelm them with our stories; we become an unstoppable wave of undeniable experiences.

When I read the essays in this book, that's what I'm reminded of—the incredible, hopeful power of survivors speaking the truth even when the world tells them they're incapable of it. And the way in which speaking that truth inspires others. Because, make no mistake, every time a survivor reads someone else's story, they get that much closer to having the strength to speak their own.

In the end, that's what this book is—an offering of strength. A show of support. A reminder that no matter how bad things get, there are so many others who have your back and understand what it is to feel fear, and rage, and trauma, and joy—sometimes all at once.

Reading each essay feels like receiving Communion, understanding the bigger picture and taking pieces of each other in the best, most relevant way.

It's books like this that help us to move forward with a clear vision of what we need: stories, truth, and most of all—each other. So read with hope, read with sadness—we're all going to feel differently when confronted with other sur-vivors' truths. But know that by doing so, just by witnessing each other's lives, we are taking small, sure steps forward.

INTRODUCTION

•

Stacey May Fowles
Jen Sookfong Lee

•

WHEN WE SAT down to write this introduction, we thought of all the detached things an editor might say about an anthology like this. That it is necessary and timely. That the #MeToo movement has pushed us all to consider sexual assault and its lingering effects in new ways. That statistics show most women have been or will be harassed or exploited or assaulted in their lifetime. That it is imperative that survivors' stories are heard by those who want to enact real change. That the responsibility lies with all of us.

These thoughts, facts, and ideas will be familiar to many. They are, of course, true and important, and we could certainly write pages and pages on them.

We could, but we didn't.

Instead, we wrote notes about a black hole, one that lives inside the body and the mind. We wrote about how it can wax and wane with time, cling to and surprise you, how it can occasionally be forgotten, until it isn't. We wrote about how that darkness can be a part of every decision, and every action, whether we like it or not. We wrote about how it can shrink and swell, can be unpredictable, debilitating, and all-consuming. How it can let you have a good day, only to take that day away.

This black hole—for the contributors in this book and for so many others—is the trauma of sexual assault.

In the years following sexual violence, many survivors learn to live differently. They learn to adapt to a trauma that attaches itself to them, building a new existence around that black hole that makes its presence known in every choice, every intimate act, every hope and dream. Its gravitational force is undeniable. Trauma makes it easy to fall in love with a person who hurts you because that's what you thought love was supposed to feel like. It whispers that you're not valuable, that your presence on this earth is expendable. It distorts your vision when you look in the mirror, just enough so that you hate what you see.

So when we sat down to write this introduction, the vital question became: How do we, survivors of sexual violence, actually endure living this way? And, more importantly, how can we—all of us—make things easier for survivors who are forced to endure living this way?

IN THE PAST few years, we have made remarkable progress in the conversation around sexual assault. Survivors have been given—or, rather, rightfully claimed as their own— high-profile venues to speak about the things that have happened to them. Many have worked hard to upend any notion that they should feel shame about what they have experienced. There have been incredible conversations about consent, education, justice, and restoration. There has been growth, and hope, and even victory in the face of so much pain.

But for us, one piece seemed to consistently be missing—how do survivors actually cope in the long aftermath of assault? The daily reality of surviving violence is not the stuff of headlines nor our collective sympathies, yet it is where some of the bravest and hardest work is done. It felt important to talk about that work and to interrogate how we might, as a culture and a community, best support it.

For many, recovery is long and it is arduous. It is even *boring* in its seemingly endless monotony, its progress in increments so tiny it doesn't feel much like progress at all. Trauma affects the way you navigate the world in myriad ways, mars the way you move through moments, the ease of which others take for granted. It defines even the minor parts of your days, long after the headlines have run and the hashtags have stopped trending. It changes your relationships, your faith in yourself, and your ability to trust and connect with the world around you. Trauma can alter you irrevocably, with recovery moving so slowly it feels like it may never end—like you'll never get "better." (Whatever that means.)

So many of our popular narratives of sexual assault seem to end with either justice or the marked absence of justice. In fiction, there is a grievous act, a perpetrator caught, and a consequence delivered. Rarely do these stories, whether real or imagined, touch on how we walk the long road that follows, and all that journey entails. The sleepless nights. The ceaseless fear. The jobs and friends and opportunities lost. The emotional, physical, and literal costs. What justice really looks like. And what it has the potential to look like.

Despite all of our recent conversations, how enlightened we collectively claim to be, a great deal of the very heavy burden of moving forward from sexual assault still lies with those who have been harmed. Yes, we are outraged, and we express our disdain, but seldom do we ask how we are collectively and continually supporting those who deal with the real day-to-day realities of trauma. We so often fail at giving space for survivors to voice those unique realities. We don't advocate for their safety and security when they speak out, nor do we make room for them to articulate what they need.

Beyond that, the systems in place to aid in healing are hard to navigate, and victims are left alone to figure them out. The pathways are riddled with cracks the vulnerable can fall through, making it hard to stay connected to community and care. What's more, there isn't a singular story or a one-size-fits-all guide to healing (if one exists at all), nor does the world make considerations or accommodations for the traumatized. Survivors face judgment, disbelief, pity, and subsequent pain, all while being expected to "get over it" and "move on."

So we felt it was important to highlight the narrative of sexual assault we're not talking about—the weeks, months, and years that follow the event. The difficulty eating, sleeping, working, or connecting with friends and family. The everyday pain and fear, and ultimately the incredible resiliency and strength. The unique and diverse forms that "coping" can take, whether considered acceptable, or branded as harmful.

We also know that very few survivors experience that journey of self-discovery we so commonly see celebrated in films or on bestseller lists—most of the time you learn how to cope while going to the grocery store, while picking up your kids, while simply being human. The big revelation or breakthrough may never happen. It often doesn't.

Every survivor has their own definition of what "recovery" means. We don't fit into neat and tidy models when it comes to traveling the way back from the experience of sexualized violence. "Recovery" is not a word that even applies to everyone. Sometimes "getting past" something actually just means living side by side with it, integrating its presence into your life, into every movement and moment. In fact, in creating this anthology, we often questioned whether this idea of "getting through" sexual assault was even possible, and if the popular perspective that one must "overcome" the past to move forward was actually helpful.

WITH ALL OF these many ideas in mind, we reached out to writers with a simple yet extremely complicated question: What got you through? We asked this question with a sense of openness, understanding that we wouldn't find the same answer twice, and knowing that what we would receive would have the capacity to change our perspectives on what it means to heal.

Was it traditional therapy? Was it a person or a place? Was it reclamation of self, or body, or mind? Was it a connection made or an interest fostered? Was there even any getting through this at all?

And we also understood the inherent vulnerability in posing this question—responding to our call necessitated writers to invite us into the very private spaces of their own healing, to share with readers those darker moments in the hope that it would make them feel less alone, that it would start a dialogue about what it means to live in the long shadow of another person's decision to violate you.

And what we received in response was an act of the highest generosity, of incredible candor and insight, and a chance to really push the conversation on sexual assault out to its most important corners.

Narratives like these are never easy to write, or to read. Yet there is a compelling social need to know that, in the world, there are others—those who have crawled away from their abusers, who feel like they have found themselves again. While we are drawn to each other to share our trauma, we are also drawn to each other to share our coping.

The concept of healing or getting better, as Leah Lakshmi Piepzna-Samarasinha points out in the essay "Not Over It, Not Fixed, and Living a Life Worth Living," is faulty. Trauma, like any chronic condition, never leaves us, and the challenge lies not in healing it but in managing its effects on our lives. In fact, the title of this anthology is very deliberate—we wanted to publish a book that centers not on abusers but on the voices of those who are simply getting through, even though that task is far from simple.

HERE YOU'LL FIND essays from survivors who have rebuilt their lives around, and in spite of, that black hole of trauma. Alicia Elliott, with silence, consciously gives it no space. Karyn Freedman throws her body into the speed and chill and physical strain of ice hockey. Gwen Benaway searches for love. Elisabeth de Mariaffi finds older women to nurture and care for her. Soraya Palmer and her sister create new worlds that are equal parts dystopia and utopia. Amber Dawn asks her chosen partners to reenact traumatic events. These are all ways of getting through, of piling up moments of joy or accomplishment or healing around the edges of this black hole, saving them for the inevitable times when the great pit yawns wide again. It's insurance, weighing the good when we can recognize it so that we know its value when we're blind to its beauty. It's how we learn to accept that getting through is our most Sisyphean task. It's how we love the person we have become.

This book says there is a way forward, even if it's not the prescribed or sanctioned one we're used to. Even if it's not acceptable, or pretty, or inspiring. Most importantly, it says that it's a way created by individual survivors alone.

Even if, yes, there is no way of truly getting over sexual assault, no way to "overcome" it, or to "recover" what has been taken, there are ways to connect that will help us through. With bravery, honesty, and generosity, these writers are creating connections from the raw material of their own experiences and making the days, months, and years a little easier for those who read their stories.

These words are a gift in a world increasingly unsafe for and cruel toward their necessity. The contributors express both bravery and vulnerability, articulating a process of reclamation in both whispers and screams. And by sharing these truths the writers have fostered hope and offered a promise that we can use what we've learned to finally make a space for healing.

WORDS LIKE "INSPIRATION" and "courage" can be insipid, sentimental, and inadequate. They are among the detached things an editor might say about an anthology like this, things that can never really do justice to the monumental acts housed within these pages. Instead, we want to say that this book makes space for a diversity of voices and experiences, offering a place for survivors to speak and be heard, and a way to continue an important conversation well into the future. This heroic act of sharing has always been what we do, whether it's in hushed tones warning others, or in public words asking for accountability. We share what we know and how we feel because it pulls us and others out of isolation, and because it creates strength in community.

And, above all else, it gets us through.

MY HAND
BECAME A FIST

·

Lauren McKeon

•

I STARTED KICKBOXING AT age fourteen, long before I was raped. It was the culmination of years of desperate wanting, of needing to make my body into something good. When I was a child, I had strange idols. Bruce Lee. Chuck Norris. Jean-Claude Van Damme. Which is to say, I had strange idols for a little girl. Or at least, that's what I often heard. I didn't have crushes on these men, though that might have been easier for people to understand. I wanted to *be* them. These men-made-weapons owed their bodies to no one but themselves. They knew precisely how to make them do and be what they wanted. And what they could be and do was amazing.

For most of my childhood, I was shy and round. All of the panes of my body sloped outward, the lines filled in with pudge. I was never a knobby-kneed kid. My knees had dimples. My knees were suggestions of angles and bones— things that might happen to my body when I grew up.

I wanted to be skinny, of course, because that is what girls are supposed to want. But more than that, I wanted to become a woman with a wicked right hook. A woman who could land a zillion roundhouse kicks, like Lee did against Norris in the epic fight scene in *The Way of the Dragon*. As a soft kid, prone to goody-two-shoes politeness not anger, it wasn't violence I wanted. It was a way to make my body powerful and in control and mine. I was chubby and female and, therefore, keenly aware that there were good bodies and bad bodies, but that both tended to get away from the women who owned them—to belong to anyone who thought they could do a better job with them.

Nor did I want to be pretty, not precisely. I wanted to do the splits like Jean-Claude Van Damme in *Bloodsport*. The iconic scene where he's suspended, each foot on a chair, the force and strength of his body defiant, impossibly keeping him upright. I wanted to do that.

ON NOVEMBER 15, 2015, in a packed stadium in Australia, Ultimate Fighting Championship star Ronda Rousey got what was coming to her. Or that's what everybody from Lady Gaga to Donald Trump would have you believe. When Holly Holm knocked out Rousey with a round-house kick to the head, people called it karma. They hated Rousey because she didn't tap gloves, a fight faux pas that's equivalent to not shaking hands or using a salad fork for dessert—and that's also apparent confirmation of her famed egotism. They hated her because she was no longer a winner, thus rendering her trash talk and her confidence instantly insufferable. Because she said things like: "Some people like to call me cocky or arrogant, but I just think, 'How dare you assume I should think less of myself?'" They hated her because Rousey was, as Trump and plenty of others put it, not "nice." And that's a terrible thing for a woman to be, particularly when that woman does things men usually do, or would like to believe they can.

So when Rousey's face swelled up like a sun-rotted piece of fruit and then hit the mat, people cheered. Because that would bring the "bitch" down a peg.

Back then, when Rousey fell, I was still self-harming, long after my first assault. *First.* That first rape broke me. But a breaking can happen more than once. When we say "break," sometimes we also say "clean"—conjuring the image of being split in half. But when trauma breaks you, there are so many pieces, you don't know where they went, or even how to look for them. You may not even know what's gone. After the first breaking, I put back what I could. I made myself into a china doll with fault lines, a teacup full of chips. I shattered more easily after that. Lost some pieces to splinters and dust. After the second, and then the third, I forgot that I'd ever been whole. Forgot what it felt like to believe that I could be. Every self-inflicted cut was a reminder of what I deserved. A way to knock myself down and down and down, to the lowest peg, and then lower still. Because, surely, that's where I belonged.

THE COLOGNE IN my first gym was tangy sweat and bleach. The decor Muhammad Ali. The floor was concrete; we had no mats. The bathroom could only be described as gross, and I cannot ever remember venturing into the changeroom, though there was one. We had speed bags, heavy bags, a barely functioning exercise bike, and a bin full of miscellaneous gloves and pads—the flotsam and jet-sam of a boxing club. The ring that became my home was at the back. I was neither fit nor coordinated when I joined. Although I'd played sports like hockey and its girl-geared cousin ringette, I didn't have the stamina for a full kick-boxing class. Or the muscles for a single push-up. Or the flexibility for a kick high enough to reach anything but a garden gnome. I was terrible. And I was in love.

What I loved about it was everything. That first class, I brought my father and my friend, who dropped out after a few months, telling me it was "fun, but..." She never fell for it in all the ways that I did. I was obsessed. I loved the *swish* sound of my silk pants when I kicked, the quick repe-tition of *dun-dun-duh-dun-duh-duh* as my fists hit the speed bag, the hiss of my exhales. I loved that we bowed before we entered or exited the floor. I loved that our instructor, who had once been in B-rated action movies, called me "killer"—as a joke at first, and then with respect. I loved the way my sash thwacked my leg as I whipped around for a spinning side kick. And, yes, I loved it when men came in cocky and left less so when they realized a teenage girl could do things they could not. I loved it when they humbly asked me how.

For years, I went to class six days a week and trained for many hours more. Inevitably, I got better. My body did what I wanted it to, moved in the precise ways that I'd always imagined. Through repetition and practice, I cre-ated knowledge within my body, I fathomed skill where there was none. There was freedom in the doing, in allow-ing myself to be what I wanted. In the end, I wasn't a gifted fighter—couldn't do what Lee or Norris or Van Damme did—but being there made me feel alive. Adrenaline rushes during exercise, sure, but the thrill was in the purpose, in the secret. In the knowing that my body could do what few expected, what few had ever planned for bodies like mine—ones meant to look good, and feel good, and be good, all outside ourselves. I used to have fantasies of saving strangers from the nonexistent criminals in my sleepy suburb. I used to have fantasies of saving myself.

Yet I rarely told anyone I kickboxed, even when I decided to train to compete; even when my arms were speckled with bruises from blocking; even when, one time, a kick got under my headgear and I had a shoe imprint beneath my eye for a week. This was before women like Rousey and Holm dominated the UFC. I didn't know a single girl in my high school who kickboxed, or boxed, and although I'm sure I wasn't the only one, I know we were rare. But it was more than that. Learning how to do this thing with my body was the first choice I ever made about who I wanted to become—the first drop in the bucket of things I would do for myself. Telling is another form of sharing, and it wasn't self-doubt or shyness that kept me from sharing this part of myself. A visceral part of me worried that if I told someone, they might try to take that away from me. I worried that they could. And about what it meant if I let them.

FIGHTING IS BARBARIC. It's violent and maybe evil and probably not something I should venerate. It begets itself; it's prone to escalation. But have you ever punched someone, or something? I will not lie to you. It's a quick and satisfying act. If you're sparring or fighting in a match, it's methodical, controlled, driven not by primal rage but something possibly more primal: the urge to win. To be better than. The punching is not the best part. I'd much rather punch a bag than a person. No, the best part is the knowing. It's knowing that you can curl your fingers in, form a fist, angle it just so, and then, with a twist and a jab, ever so briefly connect your first two knuckles with another surface. It's a hopeful knowing that they will hurt and you will not. It's walking anywhere as a woman and feeling safe, because even if they are stronger than you, you know how to do this one thing. To make your body yours.

KNOWING HOW TO hurt someone did not stop my assault. There is a movement that resurfaces every few years that advocates for women to learn self-defense to avoid being raped. It's a divisive issue. Some women argue that every tool is worth having if it can stop a rape or sexual assault. Others say we should focus our energies on teaching men not to rape, rather than teaching women how to not get raped. When we have these conversations, we account for differences in size and strength, point out techniques that can help a woman get away. We decide it's a simple equation with predictable outcomes.

What we don't account for is the way your mind can freeze your body. The way you forget that you ever knew how to do anything. The way such a violation can disconnect your core self from your body, then smash them back together again, out of sync. We don't account for what happens when it's not a stranger but someone you like, or think you could love. How your body can be trained to fight back, but this is not the fight you trained for—you can know how to punch somebody in a boxing ring, or even on the street, yet it might not matter, because this instant is incomprehensible. You can never prepare for these layers of violation.

When I was raped at age sixteen, I did not fight back. I knew how, yet all of me forgot. For a long time, the guilt rose like bile every time I heard someone respond to stories of rape, both high profile and not, with something like, "If it were me, I would have fought back." As if it were so easy to move. As if I did not wish that I could have said the same. In those moments, I would think of how I knew how to fight him off that night under the pool table, but despite all my training, my body went sluggish. We speak of fight or flight, but it was neither. There, with the rug burning against my bare and tender skin, I performed a deep descent. If I was underwater, then I was at the bottom, so far below I couldn't see anything but pinpricks of light against the inky, suffocating dark, my limbs caught in sand, not knowing if I would ever surface. Scared that when I did my life would never be the same.

I came back to fighting after. This is important: continuing to learn how to fight helped me find my way back to myself. I was not kind to my body after I was raped. I hated it for betraying me. For not fighting then, for being something that could be acted upon. I started to punish it, even though I'd just learned that nothing would stop a person who wanted to rape. I started to have the darkest hopes: that I would spontaneously combust; that I would become disfigured; that if I saw him again he would kill me, so that I wouldn't have to figure out how to live like this. But I never stopped going to kickboxing. There, I never doubted my body. There, it didn't matter how it looked, or what could be done to it, but only what I could do with it.

I practiced roundhouse kicks and side kicks and hooks and jabs and punches again and again and again. I started to go hours early, just so that I could have more time there. Our instructor lived above the club and would let me in, then leave me. Often, I'd have the place to myself. I'd pop in the club's mixed tape and do circuit training to the Commodores' "Brick House" and the Sequence's "Funk You Up." As long as I kept moving, I didn't have to think. As long as I kept moving, I could remember what I could do. For those hours, kickboxing took a thing that no longer felt like mine—my body, a thing—and helped me give it back to myself. It made it something I wanted again, even if only for a little bit. It made it something good. Something I could control, but also love. I never told anybody there what had happened to me, and there's no way they could have known, but I think most of us needed the same thing: a way to be present in our bodies. We say that fighting is violence, but here it was a kindness.

When you're a woman, the thing about training to fight—about learning any form of martial art—is that there will always be people who think it's cute, who think it's strange, who do not understand why you want to do it. These are the same people who want to see if you can hold your own against a man in the ring, who must right the gender balance and thus their world. They are the ex-boyfriends and other men who've asked me to kick them, because I couldn't possibly know how; who've goaded me at bars; who've insisted on seeing me hit a bag, because even if they've never punched anything, or wanted to, they watch a lot of UFC and have some tips, right? They are the same people who must always question when a woman does something that, traditionally, a man does, and vice versa. They are the clingers-on to the old guard. And that's why, even when I can't articulate why I fight or who I am or who I want to become, I pick up my gloves, put them on, and punch something.

That's why a woman who fights is so rebellious, even when she's not trying to be. That's why it brings me back to myself, again and again. Because with every hit, there's the consequent declaration: *You cannot tell me what my body was made for.*

HEALING IS NOT linear. When I moved up North to Yellowknife for work after university, I stopped kickboxing. There weren't any clubs to join, and even though I bought a heavy bag for my apartment, it wasn't the same. I couldn't hit it very hard—the boom of my fists would shudder through the apartments beside and below. Yet because I still had so much anger—at myself, at everything—I couldn't hit it softly, either. In the near decade since my first rape, I'd been assaulted twice more. One of them recently. Without an outward release, I turned inward, collapsing in on myself. Again. I forgot how to put my fists up. Or, more than that, I forgot that I could. During this time, I would remember what kickboxing did for me. I would look at photographs and see my body: long and lean and strong. And I would think, *That is how I made myself better*. And I would think that I could not do it again.

The thing about being assaulted more than once is that after the first time, you start to think, *This is it*. Not that it's over, but that this is your life. If the first assault did not define me, then surely this one does. I began to think that I rose to the surface only to suffocate in the fresh air. No, that's not quite right. I began to think that there was something about me that made the air suffocating, fetid. I began to think there was no longer a way to get through this. I was horrible to myself during this time. We use the word "relapse" to talk about addiction, and it's not the right word here—yet it is: I felt addicted to self-harm. I'd tell myself that I would be better to myself. I'd tell myself that if I could just go through one day without cutting, I could make it through two, then three. I'd tell myself that I could heal everything, inside and out.

And sometimes I would. But whenever the dangerous men I allowed myself to date turned abusive, I wouldn't tell them they were wrong about me. I wouldn't say no. No, I am not worthless, I am not a bitch, I am not awful and wrong and stuck-up. I would agree, and then I would cut my arm, wear long sleeves, hide the way I was now dealing with this pain. Once, a man I was with—the last man who assaulted me—used an angry fist on me, even as my own, more skilled ones, felt impotent. The next day, the bruise on my arm was so tender it hurt to reach diagonally across my desk to answer the phone at work. Later, that night, I examined it, turned my arm to get a better look at the navy welt, arching out like wings. I gingerly ran my fingers over it, reminding myself it was my fault. Then, I made swift red lines march down my skin, this time on my inner left thigh, closer to the site of my trespass.

Eventually, I moved back to Toronto, into a house across the street from a kickboxing studio. I'd walk by it on my way home and notice the billboard-sized photo of the class, and feel a pull of embarrassment every time I kept walking. It took me a year to walk inside, cautiously, as if I'd see the ghost of my more whole self. Seeing the club swirled my emotions, making them muddy. I wanted to go in. I wanted to believe that I could do it again. I wanted to believe that I could get better. Yet an anxiety had nestled into my limbs, filling my muscles, slicking my joints. It took weeks more before I went to my first class. Nothing came back to me. I felt out of sync with these yelling men, these strutting, aggressive bodies. They would make us women practice getting attacked at a club, getting grabbed by a stranger. But it wasn't make-believe. Not to me. Not to how many other women there?

After a couple of months, the instructor paired me with a man who was new to class. Mostly, the women were paired with other women, but tonight we were mismatched. I'd seen him before, this man: he walked with a cocky menace, his body slanted into a slash. His closed expression made it clear he didn't want to be paired with me, a woman. And I'd lost my swagger. Or, rather, the renewed fear of these past few years had dined on that swagger so often that it was gone. We practiced punching and kicking combinations back and forth, holding strike shields—the pads a coach or partner will hold so that you can practice hitting a human, not a heavy bag. I knew that he was hitting too hard, trying to hurt me, trying to tell me that he could, that I didn't belong there. When I got home, my breasts and torso were already blooming black.

I went back a few times after that, then stopped. I kept paying, though, for nearly a year. I didn't want anyone to know I failed, least of all myself.

A BOXING GLOVE is heavy with padding. It forces your hand into a fist, and then forces you to protect it. Take a swing and you'll feel the impact. You'll know that you struck something. You'll feel your knuckles connect, feel your own flash of not quite pain but power. If you do it right, the thing you hit will hurt more than you do. If you do it right, it will be the best thing you have ever felt. You'll feel cradled and invincible with your fists encased in twelve, fourteen, sixteen ounces of foam and leather. At first, your gloves will be stiff. You'll share the hurting with whatever you hit. Then the balance dips. And then there will come a time when, after hundreds and thousands of hits, after so many hits you will wonder how there was ever a time you did not do this, your gloves will begin to wear out. The padding will go so soft you'll hurt again, too. They will have done their job. And you'll get a new pair and begin again.

A YEAR AGO, I went back, though not to the same place. At this point, I'd been in therapy, at last, for more than a year. When my therapist asked me to think of any positive coping mechanisms I had, I could only think of one.

Fighting. This time, I did my research. I joined the Toronto Newsgirls, a boxing club founded for women and transgender people. The moment I walked in, I fell in love again. My first club was small and run by a moonlighting accountant, whereas Newsgirls is huge and run by the *coolest* woman, yet the no-frills, you-got-this vibe felt the same. Here was a fun place, but also a place where only the fight mattered—whatever it was you were fighting.

When you walk into the club, during any given class, you'll see women of all sizes and ages, women of color, Indigenous women, gay women, and trans women. You'll see women who come to learn how to fight because they are athletic and it's exercise, and women who come to learn how to fight because they need to find their way. Sometimes, like me, one becomes the other, and back and forth, and back again. But it helps just to be here. Posters and photos of fighting women (and, of course, Muhammad Ali) hang everywhere. So do clippings of all the kick-ass stuff the club has done over the years. There is also a small food bank, a library, and a piano. There are posters for theater, parties, rallies. There is nothing that says, *You will heal here,* but everything says that you will.

After several months of coming to class, of finding my path back to myself, our instructor started letting me work out with the women training to compete. I wasn't as good or as strong or as fast as them, but she must have known I craved a chance to be in the ring again. I wanted to do that dance again, the one where your body knows what it is doing and what it is meant for, even when you doubt it. I wanted to feel the singing adrenaline when it—when

I—became powerful, not powerless. And so I stepped into the ring and tried not to worry about whether I was good enough but just whether I felt good. During one recent class, I was paired with one of the top competitors.

After only a few jabs, she called a time-out. "You've done this before," she said. "I can tell."

I nodded and told her that I thought I'd forgotten how. "But now," I said, "now I'm remembering."

THE GOOSE

•

Heather O'Neill

●

A young girl is standing in the middle of nowhere.

YOUNG GIRL: I don't want to be in this story, if you don't mind.

NARRATOR: Go ahead. It will be okay.

YOUNG GIRL: I am so little. Why do I have to be so young?

NARRATOR: It's essential to the story.

YOUNG GIRL: And why do I have nothing on but a black coat?

NARRATOR: That is the jacket I was wearing when my mother sent me away from home. I've always liked pea coats.

YOUNG GIRL: I really wanted a dress.

NARRATOR: Your body does not belong to you.

YOUNG GIRL: If you decided that I should be here, then are you my mother?

NARRATOR: No, I am not your mother at all. You came from my imagination.

[pause]

You are me, I suppose.

YOUNG GIRL: Well, where am I exactly? All I can see is whiteness. Is this where you grew up?

NARRATOR: Of course not. The world I grew up in was ugly. In the 1980s everything was garbage. We wasted our time on useless discoveries. We tried to perfect things that did not need perfecting. We created a pump for your toothpaste. There was a lamp you could turn off with a clap. We created things that would break and then would be no longer worth fixing. There was garbage everywhere.

YOUNG GIRL: I like your time.

NARRATOR: It's going to be windy in a minute. It will lend a certain tangled beauty to your hair.

YOUNG GIRL: So it did.

NARRATOR: It's been bombed. It was like a city that had just been conquered. The first thing one does is fuck the virgins. That's why I'm here at wartime. It's right after the war. When the female bodies don't belong to anyone in particular. You are at once afraid of the liberators and the conquerors. It really makes no difference to you. You're going to be raped anyways.

YOUNG GIRL: Where did you find this landscape, if it wasn't yours?

NARRATOR: In a pile of plays in my high school. The pages were always coming unstuck. The pages were the color of cigarette stains. There were red and green and black date stamps in the back of the book. They were absurdist plays that had been published after the war.

YOUNG GIRL: I don't like that I'm a girl in this setting. Can I at least have a pet?

NARRATOR: All the animals have been eaten. The cats have been put on sticks and roasted over a fire. Even the rats have been eaten. There are no dogs barking. If you are worried about dogs, don't be. Everyone ate their pets. It's better to eat your own pet than to have a neighbor eat it. Everyone's a cannibal after the war. I will give you a friend. A goose.

YOUNG GIRL: A goose. What good is a goose?

NARRATOR: Here the silence is everywhere. If your goose were to start to bark, then it would make as much noise as a thunderstorm. It is very high-strung. It seems to gobble at everything it encounters. Every time there is a noise. That is a good thing. That's what you need. Someone who will speak up. Someone who will make an inarticulate racket. Someone who doesn't have to worry about language when they are communicating.

YOUNG GIRL: Oh, is this my suitcase? Why is it so light? It seems empty.

NARRATOR: The suitcase is so people know that you are lost. The suitcase is always almost empty. The suitcase is decorative. It's just a prop. Actors never have anything in their suitcases. You will have to perform the weight. You will have much difficulty pulling it down the street. That will be your performance. All that you have is your victimhood.

YOUNG GIRL: Thank you for nothing, as they say.

NARRATOR: It's not completely empty. Look inside.

YOUNG GIRL: There's a black book. With no words in it. I was hoping I could read it.

NARRATOR: Then there would be a story within a story. And what if the girl in the story you are reading found a book and she began to read that story?

YOUNG GIRL: Then there would be a story within a story within a story.

NARRATOR: Correct. And it might not even end there. It could go on like that for infinity. Like two mirrors looking at one another trying to figure out who is the reflector and who is the reflected. Who is the subject, who is the object, who is under whose gaze.

YOUNG GIRL: Can't two people look at each other, as two subjects?

NARRATOR: No. Not in this play.

YOUNG GIRL: There's also a pot. And a box of matches.

NARRATOR: So when you want dinner, you can light a fire under it and heat up your food. Are you hungry?

YOUNG GIRL: I wish you hadn't mentioned it. Now I am. You put the hunger inside me.

NARRATOR: Pull up one of these celery roots.

YOUNG GIRL: Where?

NARRATOR: Right there, by your feet.

YOUNG GIRL: Oh.

NARRATOR: Pull on it hard.

YOUNG GIRL: I'm trying, but it won't work. Look at me. All I have are these small hands and my small boots to dig the heels in the ground.

NARRATOR: Pull harder. Keep pulling.

YOUNG GIRL: I can't. It's killing me. It hurts my hands. There's no point to any of it. The roots are in too deep. They don't want to come out. No one has ever pulled one of these out before. How can I know it's even possible! Maybe I'm wasting my time here.

NARRATOR: Keep pulling.

YOUNG GIRL: I think I felt it move. It gave a little.

NARRATOR: Of course it did.

YOUNG GIRL: There it is!

[pause]

The root is alive. Look, it's wiggling around.

NARRATOR: Let's wash it in the pot, then. Give it a warm bath.

YOUNG GIRL: It's a small heart.

NARRATOR: Don't boil it. We don't want to kill it. We want it to be happy.

YOUNG GIRL: It isn't beating! Can't you see that it's dead? What will I do now? Everything is going to start falling apart. I really can't stand this.

NARRATOR: Heat it up.

YOUNG GIRL: The matches. The matches.

NARRATOR: The goose is leaning into the fire and stoking the flames.

YOUNG GIRL: It's beating.

NARRATOR: Good. When I was a child, I was crazy for chocolate with alcohol in it. I also liked cake that was soaked in rum or brandy. It tasted like I was eating the heart of a unicorn.

YOUNG GIRL: Where shall we sit to eat this?

NARRATOR: Let's go inside this room.

YOUNG GIRL: All I see is a chesterfield.

NARRATOR: A landscape in a play can be composed of very few elements. It's all about what you have available. You can just use a park bench and you will be in a park. You can put a tree in the center and you are in the middle of nowhere. You can just use a couch and you are in a living room.

YOUNG GIRL: Ah.

NARRATOR: This is the living room where it happened, you know. I was sleeping in an abandoned building I broke into. The room was beautiful. It was.

YOUNG GIRL: I can see that now. I can see why you thought you were safe.

NARRATOR: I went to sleep on this chesterfield.

YOUNG GIRL: Shall I go to sleep now?

NARRATOR: No. Take off your coat.

YOUNG GIRL: I have nothing on now.

NARRATOR: If you are wearing a blindfold, then you can't be completely naked.

YOUNG GIRL: I can't see a thing! Has the blindfold been on my head the whole time?

NARRATOR: No, I just added it now.

YOUNG GIRL: What do I do now?

NARRATOR: Read what happened to me out loud from the book.

YOUNG GIRL: I can't read with a blindfold on.

NARRATOR: It's written in invisible words anyhow. I'll put the words in your head.

YOUNG GIRL: I'm frightened.

NARRATOR: Look, you can do it. It isn't the act in itself that is ugly. It's just a physical action. Like trying to fold a ladder. Or reaching under the chair for something you dropped. Or licking envelopes and closing them. It's the feelings inside me at the time that were ugly. So go through this without emotions and you will be okay.

YOUNG GIRL: Will the man be here?

NARRATOR: What man? I have always thought about the act itself. I have always reflected on the cause. And the cause was never, ever the man. He seemed irrelevant. Society chooses its victims. I think people wanted me to be raped and strangled and thrown in the river. I saw it in the way they looked at me. Their looks of contempt. Those looks were violent. Those looks were a form of abuse.

YOUNG GIRL: Everything is a form of abuse now.

NARRATOR: Yes! But nothing was a form of abuse when I was a girl. Nothing at all. It depended on the body that was abused. You had to prove first that you were worthy of being a victim. I was not worthy of being a victim. I applied to be a victim, but my application was rejected. Because I could not be a victim, anything that happened to me was permissible. You could do whatever you wanted to my body. It was a land where there were no laws or regulations.

To hit me was not the same thing as hitting another child.

[pause]

Also, we don't need another actor. I tend to become too abstract and philosophical when I talk about abuse. Abuse has always hidden in the realm of the philosophical.

YOUNG GIRL: I just remembered, we did this yesterday. I thought I was having déjà vu, but we really have done this before.

NARRATOR: I like repetition. It is how children learn. They ask you to repeat a peculiar, amusing gesture over and over again. Until they can understand.

YOUNG GIRL: I hate a boring, pointless play that doesn't make sense.

NARRATOR: It can't make sense if it's going to make sense of the unspeakable.

YOUNG GIRL: Why does it have to be me? Why can't you make the confession? Why should it be a fictional character?

NARRATOR: As a survivor of abuse, I suppose I am de facto an unreliable narrator. In fiction everything is real. Non-fiction is a strange place of make-believe. You don't have to prove anything in fiction. I invented you in order to be believed.

YOUNG GIRL: Who do I speak to?

NARRATOR: The audience?

YOUNG GIRL: Can they break through the fourth wall? What if they speak to me?

NARRATOR: They can say anything they like. But there can be no questions. All questions are insulting. All questions are an attempt to get their narrative in. All questions are an attempt to take the driver's seat. Questions are all interrogative. They are there to accuse you of lying.

From now on, we exist in a world without questions. Only statements. It is the world of the absurd, because you will accept all the facts that you are given. Accept everything as fact. For once. For once.

No one will have any idea when your statement is coming. That is what makes it so alarming. No one is prepared. They expected it to come after a question. As though the question has all the agency. A statement without a question has all the agency. A statement without a question is very suspicious.

Here, let's take some flowers from these graves to put in your hair. People will never believe those compositions are yours. They will say it's just the suffering speaking. They will attribute that to the abusers too. We raped her. And now she speaks in the language of rape. We taught her everything she knows. She wouldn't be a thing if we hadn't persecuted her.

That's why you might as well say it is your fault. At least you will get to be the protagonist here.

MY FORBIDDEN ROOM

·

Alicia Elliott

ONCE UPON A time there was a man named Bluebeard, a man so wealthy he was able to buy a string of young wives. None of the relationships seemed to work out. Still, Bluebeard was persistent. His latest acquisition was a girl who did not want to marry him, but who was dragged down the aisle nonetheless.

Shortly after their marriage, Bluebeard announced to his wife that he must leave on urgent business. He told her to enjoy her time without him, and then handed over a ring of keys. She could use any and all of the keys, he said—all except one: a small rusted key to a closet on the first floor. He led her to the door, then warned her: "Never open this door, or you shall suffer my wrath."

Although she initially tried to resist the temptation, the young wife was eventually so overcome with curiosity that she had to open the forbidden door. Inside were the dead, mutilated bodies of all Bluebeard's former wives. As soon as he came back, he knew she'd opened the door.

"You must now face my wrath," he told her, "and join my other wives." Naturally, before he could kill his wife, her strapping brothers arrived out of nowhere and killed Bluebeard. His young wife inherited his fortune. Apparently, she lived happily ever after—whatever that means.

I've always been confused by the moral of this story. Charles Perrault, the most famous chronicler of this tale, suggests the following: "Curiosity, in spite of its appeal, often leads to deep regret. To the displeasure of many a maiden, its enjoyment is short lived. Once satisfied, it ceases to exist, and always costs dearly." This moral, which seems to warn women against premarital sex, also shames Bluebeard's wife for her curiosity. The problem with that, of course, is Bluebeard was a serial killer. If she hadn't used that key, are we supposed to believe that Bluebeard would have treated her well and grown old with her? That he would have stopped killing altogether? Somehow, I doubt it.

Perrault's failure to mention the sins of Bluebeard is suspicious, to say the least. Why doesn't his moral caution against doing terrible things that become terrible secrets? Against requiring your wife to pass a sadistic, manipulative test? Against not only murdering all of your wives but foolishly hoping their bodies will be safe in your first-floor closet forever? If the roles of Bluebeard and his wife were swapped, I have a feeling Bluebeard wouldn't be shamed for being curious. He would be lifted up as a hero: the man who bravely opened the door his wife demanded stay shut, finally revealing her as the murderous, manipulative witch she always was.

The real moral of this story—the one Perrault is too cowardly to admit—is that secrets are only allowed to be kept if they are a man's secrets. The woman who threatens to reveal those secrets will live a life of deep regret. Any enjoyment she may experience will be short lived and cost her dearly.

WHEN I WAS sexually assaulted, I didn't tell anyone. I didn't even let myself think the words "sexual assault." My bodily reactions—constant stress, crying, disordered eating and sleeping, vomiting, wanting to drink during the day and avoid all sexual contact—were screaming to me that something was very wrong, but I willfully ignored the signs, reminding myself that I was an outspoken feminist who knew all about consent. I wasn't the type of woman who got raped.

Meanwhile, the man who sexually assaulted me was sending me threats. He warned me to not tell anyone what happened. To keep his secret. I agreed. Even when I couldn't keep his secret anymore, I still kept it. I told everyone that what had happened was consensual. To this day, I've only ever told three people the truth.

It didn't matter. He was furious. He retaliated by telling my best friend at the time an awful story, the details of which I still don't know. She refused to speak to me for weeks. When she finally responded to my texts, it was only to tell me to stop texting my rapist. I hadn't messaged him in days, but he was still sending me regular death threats.

He'd warned me. Society had warned me. I didn't listen. Now I was facing their wrath.

IN THE DAYS, weeks, months, and years following my sexual assault, I've gone over the details in my head many times. I've played out alternative scenarios, tortured myself with how minutely different choices could have stopped everything. My inner logic sounds eerily similar to the logic of attorneys who represent accused rapists. I've questioned what I drank that night, what I wore, what I'd said to my rapist in every interaction leading up to that night, what I'd said to him in every interaction afterward.

The only thing that has made me feel better is actively distracting myself from remembering that night. At first, I was wary of doing this. There's a very clear stigma around repression and denial. As survivors, we are constantly told that we should face our traumas and work through them. That this is the correct way to heal. But every time I tried to sift sense from my guilt and pain, all I found was more guilt and pain. Eventually, I decided that, little by little, and as much as I was able, I wanted to forget.

I don't want this choice to be falsely characterized as denial. I'm not denying what happened to me. I can't. That night represented a break between who I was and who I've become. I can no more go back to my old self than cooked food can become raw again after it's been submerged in boiling water.

But I can stop the cycle of torturing myself.

Maybe.

I can try.

APPARENTLY, INTENTIONAL FORGETTING, even when it is done consciously, is a defense mechanism, which is somehow different from a coping strategy. I don't know exactly what that difference is. Even the study "Coping and Defense Mechanisms: What's the Difference?" by psychologist Phebe Cramer has little guidance to offer. One set of criteria used to differentiate between the two was considered to be "more a matter of emphasis than critical difference." Another, based on how they both affected psychological or physical health, was "found to be without support."

The obvious differences to me are the negative and positive connotations. Calling something a "defense mechanism" implies that the person is accidentally dealing with an issue without meaning to, whereas calling something a "coping strategy" or "coping mechanism" implies the person is actually choosing to deal with that issue. In other words: one is passive and one is active. Passivity is usually considered a feminine trait and, therefore, undesirable. Being active, however, is considered inherently masculine and, therefore, aspirational. It's strange that something like intentional forgetting, which is being done actively, is still considered a passive defense mechanism. Perhaps not as strange as giving different, arguably gendered terms to the same healing process. But we are living in a society that encourages companies to take two of the same razor, paint one pink and one blue, then charge more money for the pink one. We should probably expect this sort of thing.

CONSIDERING THE CULTURAL stigma around related concepts like denial and repression, intentional forgetting may seem to some like a bad way to heal. However, there is mounting evidence that it is, in fact, a healthy alternative to intentionally remembering. The more we revisit events, the more entrenched they become in our memory. When those events are traumatic, like a sexual assault, they have intensely negative emotions attached to them, which are nearly impossible to separate from the memories themselves. Continually revisiting these negative memories not only keeps those memories fresh, it also keeps the person remembering them from feeling good.

This is similar to the way that depression works. As Jutta Joormann, Paula T. Hertel, Faith Brozovich, and Ian H. Gotlib explain in their study "Remembering the Good, Forgetting the Bad: Intentional Forgetting of Emotional Material in Depression," depressed people have a tendency to almost continually ruminate, or reflect on, their past. This tendency to conjure up negative thoughts and memories, then dwell on them, creates a cycle of negativity the depressed person cannot seem to escape. Even when a person believes ruminating on the past is a positive way to cope with depression, they dislike how uncontrollable this method is—how despite their best intentions to keep the poisonous thoughts out, they always seem to find a way to seep back in. Those who try to solve their problems by working through their memories are often overcome by negative thoughts, which ultimately hinders their healing.

Ultimately, the authors suggest training depressed people to intentionally forget "could prove to be an effective strategy" for treating depression.

Perhaps trying to forget your trauma isn't as unhealthy as it seems.

I'M NOT ENCOURAGING sexual assault survivors to stay silent. It's very important that survivors disclose what happened to people we trust so we can get the support we need. But the amount of detail that we go into when we decide to disclose our assault should always be up to us.

It's natural to have questions for sexual assault survivors. People may even think they're doing us a favor by allowing us to tell them everything that happened. After all, the truth (supposedly) will set us free. But isn't the most important truth that we were assaulted? Isn't that enough? Or must we relive our pain in agonizing detail so that other people's curiosity is quenched?

I KEEP COMING back to Bluebeard's forbidden room. I have one, too. Instead of the corpses of former lovers, though, mine holds a memory of that night. It's projected on the wall in an endless loop. Every time I watch it, I criticize myself mercilessly, stupidly hoping that if I watch it enough times, the ending will change. It never does.

I hate this room. I hate what it holds, what it makes me feel, what it makes me think. Whenever I can escape, I lock it up tight. I pass the key off to someone I trust and try to forget any of it exists.

Just because I've handed you the key to this room, doesn't mean you should use it.

WHEN I WAS a child, my mother told me about Jesus's resurrection. She said he told his apostles he would rise on the third day after his death. When that third day came, and Jesus appeared to them in Galilee, Thomas didn't believe it was him. Who would believe something like that? It goes against all that anyone understands about the world. Jesus may have been the son of God, but he was dead. He couldn't come back.

The only way Jesus could convince Thomas he was, in fact, himself was by letting him put his fingers in his open wounds. Thomas gouged the holes where nails had pierced Jesus's hands and feet, slid his own hands inside the wide gash in Jesus's side. Only when Thomas examined the evidence of his Lord's pain firsthand was that pain finally made real to him. Only when Thomas felt the contours of Jesus's torture was Jesus himself made real to him. He had no problems believing once Jesus offered up his trauma as proof.

This story always disturbed me. I imagined Jesus wincing with pain as Thomas's hands emerged from his body dripping with blackening blood. *What kind of friend was he?* I wondered. Why did his belief hinge on such grisly proof? How did this make Jesus feel, that his best friend wouldn't believe him unless he let him violate his body?

None of these questions were answered. The fact that one of Jesus's apostles required this type of traumatizing, invasive "proof" is accepted as necessary and normal. After all, what would we expect Jesus's disciples and friends to do? Take his word for it?

I often wonder about this burden of proof. Is my pain only valid when someone who has never felt it bears witness to it? Must I be hypervigilant about my entire person, always? Making sure that my face is composed in the perfect silhouette of trauma—any hint of a smile hastily swept away—whenever I want someone to believe me? Must I forsake all joy, all warmth, to take up my role as the "perfect victim"? As if ever experiencing happiness again were somehow evidence that I never experienced agony, anguish?

Maybe this is why I've only ever told three people.

PAIN IS, AT least partially, performative. It's never just for us; it's also for those around us. In case I ever happen to forget this in my own life, I have plenty of reminders in the world around me. For example, the case of Amanda Knox.

Knox was a twenty-year-old American woman living in Perugia, Italy, who came home after spending the night with her boyfriend to find her roommate, Meredith Kercher, murdered. One of the lead detectives on the case noticed that Knox was not crying hysterically, as he assumed she would be. Instead, she was kissing her boyfriend—something he reasoned that no innocent woman would ever do after her roommate was found dead, ever. Her reaction to trauma was so far from what this detective considered the "right" response that she was considered a main suspect in the murder case.

There was no real evidence to connect her to the murder. No blood, no DNA. No motive. In fact, the evidence was so scarce, the prosecution had to concoct a ridiculous story that maintained Knox somehow killed Kercher without leaving any DNA evidence, despite the fact another suspect, Rudy Guede, left DNA all over the room. It didn't matter. Knox was still convicted of Kercher's murder and imprisoned for four years before being retried and, eventually, acquitted.

If Amanda Knox had performed her trauma properly, maybe she wouldn't have been considered a criminal.

If I'd performed my trauma properly in front of family and friends—cried openly, poured big glugs of vodka into my orange juice while they were watching, threw up on the toes of their shoes instead of in the toilet of a bathroom stall—maybe they wouldn't have been so quick to believe me when I lied and told them that I'd wanted it.

I NEVER KNOW when I'm allowed to feel my pain and when I must put it away for the sake of company. People may want me to cry in front of them initially, to "prove" myself, to make them feel a part of my pain, but they don't want to witness that proof—or pain—forever. They don't want me to start hyperventilating when an episode of *Girls* we're watching together unexpectedly deals with rape. They certainly don't want me to ruin their outing to Banff's Cave and Basin hot springs by having a breakdown when a strange man pushes past me.

These displays of pain and trauma are not cute. They're not "healing." They're inconvenient: intrusions of real-world ugliness that disrupt the collective illusion of perfect put-togetherness. Despite this idea that survivors should share, that we should remember and then move past our pain, that we should "deal" with our issues, there are very few places any of us can show our scars without being shamed. If we slip up and accidentally let our trauma overtake us in public, we are treated with shock and disdain—as though showing human emotion makes us somehow less than human.

I SUPPOSE I should stop being so surprised when victims of sexual assault are treated as less than human. After all, the dehumanization the Canadian courts allowed during the Cindy Gladue murder trial is enough to make a person physically ill. I would rather not go into the details of the sexual assault that led to her death, which are deeply disturbing. Instead, I would like to emphasize that Cindy Gladue was a thirty-six-year-old Métis woman who had three teenage daughters. She liked cooking shows, made legendary apple crisps, loved to draw and listen to Mötley Crüe. She sang Sarah McLachlan's "Angel" to her daughters to lull them to sleep. She was loving. She was loved.

During the trial, photos of Gladue's dead body were shown in front of her mother without warning, the distressing images imprinted on her mind forever. Gladue's vaginal tissue, one of the most private parts of her body, was entered into court evidence and displayed to rooms full of strangers. This was apparently what was required to convince an all-white jury that she, an Indigenous woman who performed sex work, deserved justice when she was murdered. She still didn't get that justice. The man accused of murdering her was cleared of all charges, which meant her body was further violated after her death for no reason. Her trauma was put on display in a desperate attempt to shock jury members into feeling empathy for someone they'd been told their whole lives wasn't a real person, to remind them that the accused, a white man, the type they'd been told their whole lives to make excuses and allowances for, was deserving of punishment this time instead of more excuses and allowances.

That's the unspoken truth about these pleas for our stories, and these criminal trials. They're never just a presentation of the facts. They're arguments—and one side is much easier to make than the other. Arguing to consider a woman a liar in a society that has hammered in women's inherent unreliability is not difficult at all. The story of Bluebeard and his supposedly deceptive wife is evidence of that. Arguing to believe a woman, despite this widespread myth, is much more challenging.

Similarly, arguing that a manipulative woman is making false claims of rape to "get even" with an innocent man is not hard; it's merely spitting back up the same ideas about men and women we've all been forced to swallow for centuries. But arguing that a woman deserves the right to police the boundaries of her own body—boundaries that are continually, sometimes violently, broken by men who have been taught to disregard a woman's active lack of consent—is a task similar to Sisyphus rolling a boulder up a hill, only for it to roll back down and crush him. It's contrary to all that we've been taught about women, about men. It questions the very legitimacy of misogyny, and thus, society.

In other words, it's blasphemy.

People are willing to believe anything that reinforces their unexamined view of the world—no matter how it strains the laws of physics, decency, and common sense. They'll believe Gladue consented to the sexual assault that killed her. They'll believe that Knox was a crime scene mastermind able to erase only her own DNA from a murder scene. They'll believe that you, nearly blackout drunk and crawling over train tracks minutes before, were in a perfect state of mind to consent to sex, and did. And the only way to convince them otherwise is to let them stick their fingers in your bloody wounds. Give them details you'd rather not relive. Let them see. Let them feel. Let them taste. Your comfort, consent, and mental health didn't matter before. Why should they matter now? You want them to believe you, don't you? Don't you?

Or maybe you'd prefer to just forget.

IF SEXUAL ASSAULT survivors aren't required to give consent—or allowed to refuse consent—before being called upon to recount our own trauma, what's left for us? The men who carried out this violence against us don't have to testify in their own defense, yet we have to relive our pain to prove our innocence. Our innocence is always what's *really* on trial, not these men's guilt.

I can't be sure, but I suspect men who rape don't encounter anywhere near as many questions in their daily life about what they did and why as those they raped. They don't have to watch as people evaluate every last detail of their appearance, mind-set, alcohol consumption, sexual history, actions before and after the assault, as they weigh whether or not to believe them. I suspect they don't have panic attacks or hyperventilate when people ask these questions. I suspect they don't even feel any guilt. After all, they were just doing what society has told them they have a right to do.

When I advocate for my right to forget about my sexual assault, I'm advocating for the same right my assaulter has been given. I'm advocating for people to believe me with the same blind faith. I'm advocating for the same right to move on with my life. I'm advocating for the right to be occasionally happy, to have the chance to achieve my goals, to be considered more than someone's victim. Had I taken my assaulter to court, his lawyer would have made the same argument about him: that he has the right to be happy, to achieve his goals, to be considered more than someone's assaulter. That argument would more than likely get him cleared. Even though only the sexual assault cases with the strongest evidence go to trial, only 42 percent come back with a guilty verdict. Sexual assault has one of the smallest conviction rates of violent crime in Canada.

When you take two of the same thing and paint one pink and one blue, why does the pink one always cost more?

HERE ARE OTHER morals of other stories:

Survivors should not have to live lives of deep regret for other people's actions.

A person's decision to commit a crime should never cost the survivor more dearly than the assaulter.

Survivors should not ever be expected to supply their trauma upon demand.

Healing should not have to be the same for everyone.

MY TRAUMA IS locked inside a room. I want to ask everyone to leave it the hell alone, but I worry if I even mention it, someone will break open the door and gape at my pain without my permission. Or shame me as "unhealthy" because I won't lock myself inside that room and watch myself get hurt over and over. Or torture me with the same thoughts I use to torture myself.

Or.

Or.

Or.

I deserve to hold the key to my own memories, my own secrets, my own trauma. I deserve to decide when and with whom I share that trauma. I deserve the right to say no, to move on—or not.

I deserve what my rapist never gave me: a choice.

SKINNY DAYS

•

Juliane Okot Bitek

How am I still here?

Inbox: 0 unread / 23 messages

1.   November 27, 2017
Dear Juliane Okot Bitek, We currently send you a letter when-
ever we take enforcement action on your case, as we understand
the payor may respond to our action in a way that is of concern
to you . . .

Dear Dad, because you're my father.

Dear Dad, because you're still dead and I'm looking for
a way out.

It's already November, cold, rainy, and I'm thinking
about what it means to have a father who remains dead.

What is your story of pain? they ask.

Where did it hurt most? What were those days like?
What do these dates mean to you? Why are there incon-
sistencies in your story? How can we trust you when every

version of your story is different? What was your state of mind when you wrote this? Can you repeat the story, can you repeat the story, can you tell us one more time? Can you provide dates, times, locations, and number of events? Were there any witnesses? What did you do about it? Why should we believe you?

Dear Dad, the bullshit is unrelenting.
Dear Dad, what do you think about those days?

How are you?
I'm fine. What is your story? I'm fine. Your story. I'm fine. Your story. I'm fine. Not you. Your story.

2.   November 22, 2017
Dear Juliane Okot Bitek, The Family Maintenance Enforcement Program does not have a record of being provided with a change of address since you enrolled with the program December 2, 2008...

There is no way that we can separate our experiences from the readers. What do readers know? What do they want? Your story. Your story. Not you. Your story. What are you looking at? What do you want? Your story. Your story. Not you. Your story. Readers are voyeurs. Just empathetic fucks.

3.   April 6, 2016
Dear Juliane Okot Bitek, We need to confirm your address for the enrollment of the alternate file. Once we can update our records the correspondence will be sent through the mail...

Dear Dad, nothing actually happened. Nothing, if all we have to go on are the facts.

Dad, here is the photo from that night, of him, me, and my friend. His arms around both of us. Most people comment on my smile. Could be a grimace. He invites me and my friend up to his hotel, where he's having a party. Two of us, both of us, what can go wrong? Readers are voyeurs. Just empathetic fucks.

Inside are loads of people, all manner of drinks on the table. White powder in lines. Folks in different stages of hit and high. Low lights, bursts of laughter, a red lamp under the coffee table. People's voices, mostly men. Everything in slow motion.

Anything you want, he says, with a sweep of an arm over the table before us. Anything at all. I decline with the brightest of smiles. Did you have fun? Yes, thank you, I say. Is everything okay? Yes. You happy? Yes, thank you for everything. What do you need? I'll give you everything. Contacts, money, everything you need. I'm okay, thanks. He promises an email to follow up on our conversation. He kisses the back of my hand, holds my gaze. I cannot look away. He turns from me, speaks to my friend. We know this language, us women. We catch each other's eye, get up to leave together. Thank you so much. Thank you so much. Yes, we must go now. No, not tonight. But thank you. Thank you.

What's ungracious about that? Nothing happened.

See, Dad? Nothing happened at all.

So why can I only start to breathe when we leave the room? Why is my body covered in goose bumps? Why are my hands shaking? Why can't I say anything? Why does the top of my head buzz intensely? Why do my friend and I turn to each other and ask at the same time: Are you okay? Why do we reassure each other that we're fine? Why, when all it looked like was a couple of women being offered the world?

These are the facts, Dad. Nothing actually happened.

4.   August 18, 2015
Dear Juliane Okot Bitek, Your message has been received at our office and the information you provided us has been noted on your case . . .

Dear Dad, how was it to be a man and have daughters?

Preteen: catcalls, gropes as we made our way to the market and back. Hard male hands on our budding breasts and bottoms. I love you! We walk with our heads down, ashamed of bodies we cannot control.

Older city girls, now properly teenaged: we learn to toss back scorn, cast glances to wither them to piles of dirt. Some of them look away. Others counter our Fuck off! with You wish! We spit back, Like your mother, because nobody wants to hear about their mother underneath anybody. Nobody does.

5.   September 29, 2015
Dear Juliane Okot Bitek, Your message has been received at our office. The matter will be filed for consideration...

Dad, did you ever think about what it means to swear to kill any man who touches your daughters?

What does that mean?

What is it for which you would kill a man, Dad?

What does it mean to want to kill a man who touches your daughters and never, ever have a conversation with your daughters about what it is about them that you would kill a man for?

I ask because you're still dead.

In your lifetime, none of them would dare. After you were gone, they pounced.

Dad, they call themselves friends of yours.

What are men so afraid of?

What hurt are men so aware of that they cannot imagine for their own daughters?

6.   December 26, 2014
Dear Juliane Okot Bitek, Our offices will remain closed until the new year...

Years later, the man I was married to reminded me that I was lucky to live in Canada, because if we were back home, I would see. I would know "real life."

What is "real life," Dad? Dad, did you ever intend for me to know "real life"?

Our mothers tell us that men are like that.
They say I will be okay.
They say don't worry.
This is my mantra. I'll be okay. I'll be okay. I'll be okay.

Dad, what is it to be a man with daughters?

7.   April 30, 2014
*Dear Juliane Okot Bitek, I have sent the child forms out to you
today. Thank you for your patience in this matter…*

Dad, I'm caught inside the curse of a man who said and
said and said many times: You're nothing. You're nobody.
You will never be anything.

Can you hear me, Dad?

8.   March 11, 2014
*Dear Juliane Okot Bitek, We have mailed you a Request for
Information form. We will review the circumstances to deter-
mine if the FMEP may be able to enforce child support…*

I write myself into being. I write out curses. I imagine
myself in the clear, as if nothing has ever happened. I write
text to re-create the world. I write so that the story can
reveal me to myself. I am the writer. I'm the voyeur. I'm the
reader. I am a joker. I'm my own empathetic fuck. I want to
be real.

How am I today?

9. February 13, 2014
Dear Juliane Okot Bitek, Your message has been received at our office and the information you requested has been noted on your case...

Dear Dad, I have to relax my body against a strange man's chest because he says he will never let me go unless I say I love him. What can I expect when he calls me a liar because he says I wanted him, too? How is it wanting when I was thinking all the while that he might kill me if he thought different? Dad, who will believe me? Who?

Some men's hands are hard on me. Some men are cold, like concrete.

10. January 6, 2013
Dear Juliane Okot Bitek, Thank you for your message. The payor contacted our office last month and indicated that he was going to file a court application to address the ongoing maintenance...

Dad, second day in the women's shelter, a message is sent for me to go to the office.

How are you? I'm fine.

Is your room adequate?

May I call you Juliane? Sure.

Do you need anything? No, I'm fine.

Good. Please let us know immediately if you need anything. Okay?

I want you to know that you're safe here. Nobody will hurt you. But we do need to go over some paperwork. Are you okay to do this right now?

Oh, yes, I'm okay. Of course I'm okay. I'm okay.

My rib hurts. My thigh is sore from where he kicked me, Dad. The doctor says she cannot see any signs of bruising. Dad, she looks at my skin with a flashlight.

Where are you, Dad? What does it mean to be the father of daughters?

11. November 22, 2013
Dear Juliane Okot Bitek, Thank you for your message. The program has not received any funds to send to you...

Now there is a crisis of Sexual Assault in Hollywood. Capital *S* and *A*, because this is a crisis, a "newly shocking time to be alive." Every day, another rich white woman reveals her experience. Everyone gawking and sucking their mouths as if this is new. As if we were never there. As if anything will ever change what already happened.

His arm around me. Him telling me that he wants me to stay with him forever, telling the woman across that he will take care of me. Buying drinks all around. For everyone. Even the one across at the other table. A shot of vodka for all of us. The waiter scurries away, returns. The woman across wears a tight smile on her face. She accepts the drink with grace. Her eyes are hard when she looks at me. I know that she knows.

Dad, these are the facts.

12. September 18, 2013
Dear Juliane Okot Bitek, Any funds received over and above the monthly maintenance amounts are applied to the arrears owed to you...

Does an account of sexual assault include the therapist who said I had no signs of trauma?

13. June 20, 2013
Dear Juliane Okot Bitek, Your message has been received at our office and the information you...

My girlfriend says I'm lucky that I can attract men, even after all this. She says men look at me. She says no one looks at her. She says she would jump any man who looked at her.

What is my problem? It's not as if my bed ever gets cold.

The woman across from me takes the shot, touches her mouth with her eyes shut, then stands up. She brushes my shoulder as she walks by. Thank you, she says to him. He does not respond. I need to go.

14. May 28, 2013
Dear Juliane Okot Bitek, Your message has been received at our office. At this time your file will continue to be monitored closely...

Where do you think you're going? the man asks. You're mine now. We can be together. We will be very happy, all of us. You, me, and my wife, all of us. You, me, and my wife. Does the wife have any say in this proposal? I don't know. I want to leave. I can't. I can't go home.

My friend says I'm lucky that powerful men take notice of me. So lucky, she says.

How are you?

15. May 9, 2013
Dear Juliane Okot Bitek, Thank you for your message. Our records show that you received a payment of $524 on February 27. This was your regular monthly payment that was due on February 15…

What are your strategies?
How do you cope?
What is your story of sexual assault?

16. May 7, 2013
Dear Juliane Okot Bitek, Thank you for your message. The program has not received any funds to…

What is it to be shocked by the allegations of sexual assault in Hollywood?

The aunties ask why I cannot hold on to a man.
What's the matter with you? they ask.
Marriage is not easy, they say. Men are shit. You have to put up with a lot. You think we would still be married if

we got excited by all men's shit? You have to be patient. Be patient, my girl, the aunties tell me. Be patient.

17. May 6, 2013
Dear Juliane Okot Bitek, Thank you for your message. The payment of $674 received on April 9 was applied toward the payment due on March 15 . . .

Year after year after year, mail to remind me. That I am nothing. That I get to be jerked around by power at every level: Dear Juliane, Dear Juliane, Dear Juliane. I am a useless fuck. I am nobody. Still, they tell me, so lucky to live here.

18. April 11, 2013
Dear Juliane Okot Bitek, Thank you for your message. The program has not received any funds to send to you . . .

Dad, a decade before the term "date rape" was coined, a workmate offered me a ride home after the Christmas party. You want to come in for a minute? I forgot something, he said. No, I'll wait in the car. Don't be silly. Come see where I live, he said.

In the Christmas party photo, I'm wearing a short, tight red dress. We pose together in front of the Christmas tree. We sit at the same table. I have a happy smile. He has a happy smile. His arms around me, so respectful. It was in the days of should have known better should have known better should have known better. I bought the dress on sale and waited and waited and waited for December. In the photo, nothing has happened yet.

I'm told that maybe he loved me. That maybe he wanted to show me how much he was attracted to me. I'm told that men are like that. Why don't you ever go to the work Christmas party? friends ask me.

How are you?

Dad, are all men like that?

A decade after, language catches up.

Law defines date rape as a crime. Too late, the police say. We're so sorry, they say. Statute of limitations. Nothing we can do, the police say. There's no reason to question this, no doubt about the veracity of that statement. There's no reason to think that they had lied.

Once, I saw a pair of soiled white panties at the steps of the Student Union Building at the University of British Columbia. I don't know whose panties they were, or why they were there. Never heard anything.

I'm looking for language, I'm looking for language. I'm a writer. I'm a reader. I seek language that reveals itself as it lassoes back to the soiled panties, and forward to this moment.

Nothing makes sense these days.

I can't remember actual dates. This one was a work Christmas party. We took a picture together in front of the brightly lit Christmas tree. I can't remember his last name. I only know what he looks like because I have a photograph of me and him at the party.

I'm okay.

19. April 9, 2013

Dear Juliane Okot Bitek, Thank you for your message. As previously noted, the payor has a full month's time to send in a maintenance payment...

The payor makes a claim to be the receiver.

The payor told me years and years and years ago that I was nothing, nobody, would never be anything.

The payor fills out a form so that I have to pay him child support.

The institution works. The institution works within the law.

I pay child support.

I pay child support for years and years and years.

The doctor cannot see any signs of bruising.

The therapist cannot see any signs of trauma.

Dad, how do you stay dead?

20. July 22, 2012

Dear Juliane Okot Bitek, Your message has been received at our office and the information you...

The worker at the shelter goes over the house rules and asks me to sign if I agree with them. Sign here, here, and here. She reminds me that this is not a holiday. If I have a job, I need to keep going to work. She reminds me that there is no free childcare, that I should keep my child with me at all times. She hands me a package of forms to fill out for housing. She reminds me that this is my responsibility.

That I should not expect to stay here indefinitely. But I'm safe here, she reminds me also. I'm safe, and that's all that matters.

How do I cope with sexual assault?
I'm okay.
How are you?

21. August 29, 2011
Dear Juliane Okot Bitek, Please continue to report any payments for child support and the child support arrears that you are receiving directly from the payor...

Dear Dad, when I got married, people said that you would have loved to have been there. They said it was a pity that you were not there to see me so happy. We had a toast. Your former student bought champagne. We toasted you.

22. March 15, 2011
Dear Juliane Okot Bitek, Your file is coming up for review at which time the Enforcement Officer will be looking to see if the file is current (payments being made) or not current (no payments being made). Additionally, she will be interested in knowing if any changes have arisen from dealing with the Family Justice Centre...

Dear Dad,
Today was a sunny day with a rainy evening, like many, many before. Forget the past, they say. Forget the past.

A woman walks into the coffee shop where I sit looking for words. Hey! The two men sitting at the table next to mine greet her. She leans to hug one man. As she leans toward the other man, his arm slides along her bottom. Then his hands move up and down the inside of her thigh. He stops at her calf.

Is this the kind of touch that you would kill for?

All these men in the world, Dad. All of them still alive, and you still dead.

My friend tells me that she has resorted to social media to look for men. There are no real men in this city, she says. All the good men are gay, she says. I tell her that social media can't work for me. Readers are voyeurs. Readers are assholes. She swipes right and left, right and left, right left right left. She shares stories of her exploits. Vicarious living, she and I. Men and no men. Assholes or unavailable men.

How do you cope with a history of sexual assault?
Are women finally claiming their full sexual power?
Has the tide turned?
Dad, how are you?

23. March 27, 2011
Dear Juliane Okot Bitek, Your file continues to be monitored closely...

Just a little bit, your lawyer friend said, Dad. It won't hurt. I won't hurt you. I can't hurt you.

Your friend, the lawyer, the family friend. He laughed at me. You're funny, he said. Relax, there's no one here.

Everyone has gone home. Nobody will hear you shouting. Okay. Okay. Shhh. Relax. Relax. I won't hurt you. He's also dead now. Did he tell you?

What gets me through since then? What gets me through since all the thens? What gets me through the times I still don't speak of? What gets me through stories of rape, like mine, like others? What gets me through skinny days when the slice of daytime coincides with the bus ride back home, and it's cold and wet for months on end? What gets me through *You're not good enough, you're not good enough, will never be any good*? What gets me through faith-lessness, a dead father, women who want to remind me of my place, my place, my place on my knees? What gets me through the ticking of time toward the beyond?

Of what use is a dead father?

THE SALVATION IN MY SICKNESS

·

Kai Cheng Thom

•

Illness is the night side of life, a more onerous citizenship.
Everyone who is born holds dual citizenship, in the
kingdom of the well and in the kingdom of the sick. Although
we all prefer to use the good passport, sooner or later
each of us is obliged, at least for a spell, to identify ourselves
as citizens of that other place.

—SUSAN SONTAG, *ILLNESS AS METAPHOR*

ILLNESS IS A red thread that coils through my muscles and veins. It's a dark moth that flutters through my window at night and alights on my chest while I'm sleeping. It's a shadow with no fixed shape. Its fingers are cold against my throat, my breasts, my cheek. It follows me everywhere, whispering my name.

It isn't easy for me to write anymore. Once, it was no problem to whip off a three-thousand-word essay—I wrote my first novel in less than a month. I could sit on the sofa and write all night about being a survivor, a trans woman, a racialized woman, a Good Intersectional Feminist™. Then, in the morning, I would go to work or class for up to nine hours straight. On the weekends, I went to community organizing meetings or protests or political workshops. I was Supergirl; model minority extraordinaire; to use the words of trans advocate and actress Laverne Cox, a great "possibility model" for all the young activists and trans girls of color. I was all the buzzwords. I was a "good" survivor.

Now when I stare at a screen for too long, my brain fills with fog, and my face and neck go numb. My vision swims and my head spins. Pain radiates through my chest and stomach and lower arms. Talking to people or being in crowds is even worse—I get migraines and muscle tremors that last for hours, sometimes days, which sucks because I'm a social worker and a performing artist. Writing and talking and being with people is my livelihood. It's all I really know how to do.

Because horror on Earth is real and it is every day.
It is like a flower or like the sun; it cannot be contained.

—ALICE SEBOLD, *THE LOVELY BONES*

I DON'T REMEMBER the first time I was assaulted. My memories of childhood and adolescence blur together with memories of coercion, humiliation, aggression, like ice melting into a glass of water. The life of a little faggot Chinese boy (the terms "transgender," "gender creative," and "gender nonconforming" didn't exist for the community of Asian immigrants I grew up in) was full of overt and subtle violences. I took it for granted that my body did not belong to me, that there was something inherently shameful about the way I walked and talked and dreamed.

So I was not surprised or particularly horrified by the strange games my male family members played, such as the one where an adult relative would chase me down and pin me beneath his body so tightly that I couldn't breathe. Sometimes, I think I remember him rubbing his crotch against my four-year-old, six-year-old, eight-year-old body, but the memory is hazy, uncertain.

I took it for granted that my first conscious sexual experience was with my camp counselor, a white boy in his twenties, when I was in my early teens. I was not shocked or unnerved when he told me that the jagged scars on his wrists were from the time he attempted suicide after beating his ex-girlfriend so severely that he put her in the hospital.

And I took it for granted that the "queer community" that I ran away to as a young adult was full of its own hidden violence: The boy who pinned me down and fucked me until I bled. The random girl who came up behind me at a punk party and strangled me. The boyfriend who screamed and punched walls and twisted my wrist until I heard the bones pop. It did not occur to me that this was wrong, that I didn't deserve it, that anyone should care. Because no one did.

In my clinical training as a therapist, I learned that one of the classic definitions of trauma is "a life-threatening or horrifying event outside the range of normal human experience." But the things I experienced were not outside the range of normal human experience for a trans girl of color, and they were not a single event. They were a recurring theme, a litany of painful but apparently ordinary life experiences, as I suspect they are for many people who do not fit the narrative of the "good" survivor, scripted as it is to center white, middle-class, cisgender women.

Physical, sexual, and emotional violence are distinct and morally loaded concepts in the universe of middle-class white women and university-educated queers, but in the cramped world of my childhood, they were not. They were unfortunate things that happened, ethically neutral events, like the shaking of an earthquake or the howling of the wind.

IT'S A WORKDAY morning, and I am staying home to lie in bed and stare at the ceiling. My parents would be horrified. Employment, overachievement, and making money are the only safety they have known. A part of me echoes with their fear: as a social worker with a full-time job, I'm economically better off than most trans women I know. But still. Jobs don't come easily to girls like me—nor housing, nor health care. If I lose this gig by taking too many days off, how will I get another one? Social work agencies aren't exactly climbing over each other to hire trans girls.

Pain and nausea flare like electric shocks through my brain, chest, spine. There is poison dripping through my nervous system. I am at once full of anxious energy and weighed down by thick, red fatigue. I don't want to be alone.

I pick up my cell phone and dial.

"Hello, you've reached the sexual assault hotline." The volunteer on the other end speaks in sweet, soothing yet crisply articulated, unaccented English. I recognize the dulcet tones of a professional, probably white, social worker. I hate this anonymous stranger automatically.

"Is there anything you'd like to talk about?" the volunteer asks.

I don't say anything for several interminable seconds. I volunteered on a sexual assault hotline once.

"Hello?" The voice is carefully patient, encouraging but not anxious.

"Are you a white woman social worker?" I ask.

"Um... not all our volunteers are, but I happen to be, yes," she says, clearly uncomfortable with the question. "Is that important to you?"

"Sorry," I say. "I'm being difficult. I don't mean to be. I guess I'm a bad survivor."

"What makes you say that?" she says.

I take another excruciating pause. "Well," I say, "I'm not getting better."

I am too sick to write this article.

—PORPENTINE CHARITY HEARTSCAPE,
"HOT ALLOSTATIC LOAD"

WHEN MY BODY broke down, I had completed three university degrees by the age of twenty-five, all on scholarship. I was a nationally known performance poet. I had three books—a novel, a poetry collection, and a children's book—accepted for publication, and I was an online microcelebrity known for writing viral essays about race and gender politics. I was accustomed to being "excellent," because I didn't know any other way to live—like my parents before me, I had absorbed the model minority ethos, the imperative to be three times as good as everyone else because there is no other choice.

So I was also heavily invested in the story of myself as a "good" survivor of sexual assault, often without being really aware of it. But there I was: accomplished, acclaimed. A darling of the LGBT arts and activist scene. And people loved me for it, or so they said.

Every week, sometimes every day, for years, I got emails and social media messages and "friendship" requests from people I didn't know, telling me how important I was to them as a trans-woman-of-color example of survivorhood. They told me their own intense, terrible stories of struggle. They asked me for help and friendship that I couldn't give.

Recently, I was internet stalked and harassed—emailed and messaged incessantly, for days—by a trans woman living in a different country, whom I had never met, who demanded that I speak with her about my experiences of assault. She had read my writing, she said, and I was the only one who could understand her. I owed it her, survivor to survivor. By refusing to engage with her, I was perpetuating her abuse.

The art of being a "good" survivor in the eyes of the public is more complicated than it first appears. Much has been written in popular feminism about the silencing of survivor/victim narratives of sexual assault. Less attention has been paid to the opposite dynamic, which is the compulsion to speak: In order to receive validation and protection, the survivor is required to tell her story—over and over again, for the education and titillation of an audience of so-called supporters (and, of course, detractors). She must use the words "assault," "abuse," and "rape." She must fit herself—her body, her life story—into the narrow parameters of the "good" survivor narrative, like Cinderella's stepsister cutting off her toes to fit into the glass slipper.

The third-wave feminist maxim to "believe survivors" requires the survivor to first tell a story, to perform a role in exchange for care. By going public with her story, a survivor may receive support, care, acclaim, financial compensation, but she might also be rejected and exiled from her community.

In turn, the survivor becomes a personality for consumption, a political symbol for use in debate. The more sensational or cathartic the story, the more validation the survivor receives, so long as she remains within the bounds of social acceptability: Self-righteous, but not self-aggrandizing. Angry, but not overly aggressive. Upset, but not insane. She must put trigger warnings on herself. She must provide all the details. She must give of herself endlessly, must be an impeccable ally to all other survivors, no matter how different their experiences may be. Above all, she must eventually get better. She must rise above.

This is survivorhood as performance under capitalism. It leaves no room for the kind of silence that is healing, for relationships that are authentic, for stories that are complex. It demands the objectification of survivors, holding them to a standard of behavior and political correctness that is impossible to maintain.

When my body broke beneath the weight of the "good" survivorhood I had created for my safety, I could no longer be used in this way: I couldn't perform the role of survivor for others. I couldn't continue producing, speaking, living my life as a political object, as that trans-woman-of-color survivor with the pretty words. I was released, for the first time, from the imperative to be good, to be functional, to be sane.

My sickness saved me.

Traumatized people chronically feel unsafe inside their bodies: The past is alive in the form of gnawing interior discomfort. Their bodies are constantly bombarded by visceral warning signs, and, in an attempt to control these processes, they often become expert at ignoring their gut feelings and in numbing awareness of what is played out inside. They learn to hide from their selves.

—BESSEL VAN DER KOLK,
THE BODY KEEPS THE SCORE

THERE ARE SOME things that the body knows for certain, even when the mind has been convinced otherwise: It knows when it is in pain. It knows when it is hungry. It knows when it is tired. The body knows when it has been harmed. The body knows when it has to stop.

For years, I silenced my body, closed myself to the language of its guidance and cries for protection, its tenderness and capacity for healing. Like my family before me, survivors of famine and war, of bloody revolution and migration and systemic racism, I placed my faith in the twin gods of endurance and work. I think of my ancestors, peasant farmers in a rural China ravaged by civil war. I think of my grandfather, a prisoner of the Japanese during the Second World War. I think of my grandmother, schizophrenic and unable to speak English in 1950s Canada. I think of my parents, born into poverty in the country our people used to call Gold Mountain for its supposed vast riches and opportunity, in truth an often discriminatory nation born out of colonization and the attempted genocide of Indigenous peoples.

What choice did they have but to live outside their bodies? What choice did I have but to live outside mine? Haunted by the past, my family pushed past the limits of our physical selves in an attempt to secure the future: We worked harder. We went without sleep. Our bodies kept the score. The stories of those who came before resonate with my own, harmonizing in a minor key deep within the hollows of my bones.

For most of my sexual life, penetrative intercourse caused me agonizing physical pain. Most of my partners ignored this, and to be fair, I rarely mentioned it. I believed there was something wrong with me, something shameful and disgusting, which I could overcome by trying harder. When I was twenty-one years old, a friend of a friend demanded that I let him into my house, my room, my bed. I didn't want to, but he insisted. He pinned me down while I struggled silently, and fucked me till I bled. I said nothing, made no sound. Endurance. Work. I thought it was my fault for letting him in, for not saying no. Inside me, there is still a scar.

Now, I realize what my body was trying to tell me, for all those years: *This is not all right. This is not what you want.*

My body was saying, *This is not what love feels like.* My body was saying, *No.* My ancestors were saying the same thing, deep inside my bones.

I knew too much
    about myself to stay alive. I stayed
alive. I wrote names on my body with
    pins, nails, knives, fire, anything
that would mark the flesh.

—JOSHUA JENNIFER ESPINOZA,
"I AM DRAPED IN HEAVENLY SKIN"

A BODY CANNOT be violated if it does not exist. This is the predicament that trans women survivors find ourselves in, perceived as we are by most of the world as men in women's clothing, mentally ill, predatory wolves hidden among the pure fleece of cisgender femininity.

As a result of this erasure, trans women are barred from traditional "safe" spaces for women, such as most women's shelters, feminist organizing and sex workers' organizations, and women's health centers. Even those spaces that admit trans women are frequently unequipped and unwilling to accommodate trans women's actual needs, adopting flimsy "inclusion" policies rather than radically reorganizing the ways support and care are delivered.

Yet feminism stands to learn a lot from the experiences of trans women, right down to the conceptualization of sexual violence itself. Whereas it is certainly true that cis women survivors are unjustly required to fight to prove that they have been assaulted, trans women must fight to prove that we can be assaulted at all—a by-product of the myth that men or "male bodies" are not capable of experiencing sexual violence. As a result of transmisogyny—the intersection between transphobia and misogyny—trans women are thus at greater risk of sexual assault while simultaneously categorized as sexual aggressors.

Trans women must appear extra feminine, extra pure to fit the narrative of the "good" survivor. We must have all the right opinions and say all the right things, all the time. We cannot be messy or crazy or conflicted, which is to say, human. We must perform our pain for everyone around us, using the words they have chosen for us, while constantly downplaying and apologizing for our transness.

This highlights a weakness in the essentialist categories that popular feminism has participated in creating: the man/woman, perpetrator/survivor binaries fail trans women, as well as male survivors, lesbian survivors, gender nonbinary survivors, and everyone else who does not conform to the rigid standards of survivor identity politics. The truth is what all of us know, have always known, in our hearts: All of us can be violent. All of us can be hurt.

The body needs no proof. It does not need words or that thing we call "justice." The body is its own proof, its own analysis, its own justification. Panic attacks, nightmares, chronic pain, chronic fatigue, hypervigilance—this is the language that the body uses to tell its story, a language that needs no external listener to validate its truth.

*You do not need a psychiatrist to do this. A psychiatrist does
not want you to wake up. He tells you to dream some
more, to find the pond and pour more tears into it. And really,
he is just another bird drinking from your misery.*

—AMY TAN, *THE JOY LUCK CLUB*

SICKNESS CAME SLOWLY, like the seasons gradually
changing in the sky. It took me years to notice my body
speaking to me, trying to tell me the secrets that I had
denied my whole life: The anxiety. The breathlessness. The
tremors. The muscle aches. The exhaustion. The brain fog.
The lightning bursts of inexplicable rage. Little by little,
the icy palace of my "good" survivor life began to crumble
beneath the weight of my sickness.

And then suddenly, incontrovertibly, I was no longer available for production or consumption. I could no
longer give sixty, eighty, a hundred hours a week to "the
movement." I could not spend all my time at protests
or workshops or meetings, or what little extra money I
made on grassroots crowdfunding campaigns. I could not
respond to dozens of emails and messages a week from desperate people I had never heard of. It didn't matter what
other people thought of me, or what I thought of myself. I
was not able to do these things anymore. I was disabled.

Now, when my body speaks, it screams. Chronic pain
shuts my physical systems down when I can no longer
work, talk, give care to people. Chronic fatigue forces me
to sleep when I have surpassed my limits of wakefulness.
Panic and sensory overload are constantly vigilant alarms

that warn me, loudly, when my social boundaries have been crossed.

I spend more time alone now, lying down, in silence. I spend time daydreaming; going on slow, gentle walks and curling up with my boyfriend; hanging out with my close friends; eating and talking. Sometimes I spend whole days doing—horror of horrors—nothing. It's what I have to do.

My body knows, has always known, what I need. It has always tried to defend me, to protect me, even when I have silenced and shamed and disbelieved it. Even when I have not loved my body, my body has always loved me. Now my body shakes and echoes with the reverberations of my trauma and the trauma of my ancestors. This too, I know now, is a gift.

MY BOYFRIEND IS the first person I have ever dated who has really seen me, seen me without looking for something he could exploit or worship or destroy. My boyfriend looks into my eyes and does not see a survivor, but rather a smart, pretty girl he wants to hold in his arms. Still, I hide parts of myself from him. I do not want him to see the wild, wounded thing that lives inside. It doesn't matter, of course. He will find it anyway.

We are lying in bed together, and little by little, our kisses turn into caresses turn into foreplay turn into sex. He smells like clover and grass in the sun. His skin is silky on mine. When he asks if he can enter me, I tell him yes, a yes truer and more enthusiastic than I have ever given after a lifetime of boys. Boys with eyes and hands like a forest of thorns, always reaching for more. Boys who say they love you so that you'll lie still for them. Boys who use you and hurt you and throw you away like garbage.

He starts to fuck me, and for all the love he feels, it still hurts like a wound tearing open. I start to count my breaths and wait for it to be over, a trick I've known since I was a child. To my wonder, he stops and asks me what I want to do. This has never happened before. What do I want? To stop or continue? I want to be strong. I want to be good. I want to be fuckable. I want to be safe. I do not know. I do not know.

In the space made by his silence and my closed eyes, my body finds the answer. The sickness says, *Go slowly.* The sickness says, *Be careful.* It says, *All things are possible in time.* I open my eyes. Pain and desire give me the words.

"I want to go slow," I say.

All that you touch, you change.

—OCTAVIA BUTLER

MOST OFTEN WHEN I tell people that I am sick, they say, "I hope you get better soon." Sometimes phrased in the imperative: "Get better soon." I used to hope for this, too. The politics of the "good" survivor have turned survivorhood into a hopeless race to a receding finish line. Who can be the best survivor? The most articulate, most virtuous, most righteous?

What would it mean to get better? To return to the way I used to be? And what way would that be, exactly? To before I got sick? Before the last assault? Before the first, which

I can't remember? Or does it simply mean regaining my ability to work all day and night, to conform to every contradictory standard of appearance and behavior and speech that is applied to trans women who have lived through violence?

I don't want to be better. I don't want to be good. I don't want to be likeable. I want to be free.

When your body stops being useful to capitalism, it is discarded or destroyed. When a survivor stops being useful to "the movement," they are also thrown away. Illness is frightening, and threatening, because it tears away the illusion that if one just tries hard enough, then recovery is around the corner. Illness and disability expose the idea of recovery as an oppressive concept: if we are bound by the demand to be healthy, then health becomes tyranny. If we are free to be ill—to be imperfect—then we are free to be human.

I AM WRITING this essay at night. It has taken me several sittings of a few hours each. I suppose this means I have not "gotten better," or at least that I am still not as efficient, as productive as I used to be. A red paper lamp glows softly in the corner of my room. Pain flares through my spine. My throat is dry. I need water. I need sleep. There will be no more writing tonight. Illness has taught me this, has given me a different kind of strength: the strength to put myself first. This is what survival means to me now: loving myself like I have loved everyone else.

WHEN I WAS child, I used to escape from my parents' house and sit on the swings in a dilapidated playground in

East Vancouver. Sometimes bats would flutter overhead, and coyote mothers would wander by with their children. And I used to think about what life would be like when I grew up: There would be books, I thought. And friendship. There might be love that burned like a falling star. There would be a door that locked, a room all my own. A place I could enter or leave at any time.

There was a shadow beneath my skin, even then. It whispered in a silent language that needed no words. It spoke of ancestry, of weakness that is strength, of a truth I was not yet ready for.

I hear it now. I understand.

WEAVING A PATH
TO HEALING

•

Elly Danica

•

WOULD NOT HAVE made it through without rage. Rage against how I was treated, rage against the assumption that as a female I was automatically meant to be a victim of men or boys. Rage against the father who believed that female children were there to provide him with the income and lifestyle that he aspired to.

But rage that intense has a great cost. According to my family's narrative, I was a deluded, ungrateful liar. I grew into a young woman who could not cope with her "loving" father, and who lied or made up things about what happened in the basement of the home on Saturday nights. What an imagination I had, they said. Of course you must obey him—he stands in for God the Father and would do nothing wrong. This is love, they said.

Really, rage at all this was essential. It is not normal to be pimped by your father and then gaslighted by him when you complained. It is not normal to be denied food, which there was never enough of anyway, as a punishment for being uncooperative. It is not normal to be prescribed Valium for your "bad attitude" to the father.

My focus then was to punish myself—that was certainly much safer than challenging the father. He promised me that he could kill me, and demonstrated how he would do it, if I did not do as I was told, and do it willingly with a smile on my face. I did not want to die as a child, and for a child, the father is all powerful.

I now see that growing up Catholic explains a lot. My mother was initially pious. The father believed that meeting the form by showing up at Mass every Sunday would prevent scrutiny of his nefarious activities. Consider my role models: pale adolescent saints, angry nuns, and my languishing, sad mother.

The saint most in favor at that time was Saint Bernadette of Lourdes. If fighting the father was going to get me killed, then holiness would be my next-best option. I would be holy and pure. I would talk to the Virgin Mary and Baby Jesus. I would offer up my suffering for the souls in purgatory by doing what the father told me to do, though I thought that might kill me, too. It is beyond humiliating to flatter and grovel before a tin-pot dictator who thinks he is a god. This was hard work. I quickly slid back into rebellion and tried to preserve a bit of dignity. I thought too much about dying and imagined every sort of accident and illness to take me out of the father's house. I was nine when this began, and it ended too many decades later.

So many of the nuns I met growing up were desperately unhappy with their lives. They seemed bent on making the lives of their charges as miserable as possible, just because they could. It was the only power they had. It is a wonder to me that they were not all twisted. The willing and kind ones had obviously been trained in self-sacrifice from an early age: they were the dutiful daughters, the smiling victims, not the glowering, rebellious, spitting ones.

Wherever did I learn to rebel? How could I learn rebellion when my mother certainly never modeled that for me, nor did any female person I knew of then? The women in my childhood and adolescence seemed to me so many doormats, subject to the whims of "their" men. It was considered noble to be the good wife, whose preordained role in life was devoted only to pleasing the lord and master husband. I could not understand why it had to be this way, and I said so. One was not allowed to question all that was right, good, and beneficial for the fathers domestic and religious.

Patriarchal men, it seems, are so afraid of the power of women they will do almost anything to keep us from connecting to it. They like to start on us young, to make their world view seem normal. If we have the spirit to rebel, they will try to stomp it out of us.

Women in every culture pay a high price for rebellion. Poverty is a standard means of social control of women. You can't leave a bad situation if you have no money. You can't plan a future for yourself and your children while living in desperately awful and inadequate housing. You can't even think clearly when you are constantly hungry and worried about how you will feed your kids something other than noodles and mystery meats.

So if you are bent on rebellion, as I was as a young woman, you know it will mean poverty on a grand scale. I was determined to chart my own course, and poverty was a better option for me than anything else I could see at the time.

I married young to escape. But I wanted to make things, to write, to weave, to spin yarn, and to paint. As a married teenager, I could not do these things without either begging for money or manipulating household finances. It was humiliating to grovel for money because I had no right to it as a married woman. I'm talking twenty dollars, not hundreds or thousands. So I walked out of my marriage with no money and no plan.

Rebellion became a theme, a lifestyle, even when it didn't work worth a damn, even when it resulted in absolute chaos and danger. Fear is a potent motivator. But rage eventually made me bitter and toxic. I could never seem to find a way to be even moderately happy, and certainly never content. I never doubted, well into my adulthood, that the father could find ways to hurt and harm me. I never really felt safe until he was dead.

The only place I ever felt somewhat safe was in church, so at age twenty-eight, in 1975, I bought a deconsecrated United church for $300 with a friend. The church had no windows, no electricity, no heating, and no plumbing. But it still seemed like the best place for me to "get it together." And it felt safe. Cold, primitive, yet safe.

And there I began the long, long process of coming to terms with my childhood and its continuing impacts on my life. I needed to find out who I was, why I was in so much pain all the time, why I felt so damn crazy and out of control. Why I was so livid with rage most of the time. Why I hated myself, could not nurture or be kind to myself. Why I felt so worthless and awful.

I set myself the project to figure it all out. I would create beautiful things to make money, and I would write my way through.

SO THERE I was: wrapped in as many warm layers as I could manage and still move, curled up in a big thirties-style overstuffed armchair with my giant sketchbook (if the notebook was big, the writing in it would be important) and a fountain pen, writing for sometimes all my waking hours. I took breaks to pour more coffee, make toast, and cook now and then. I wrote and wrote and wrote.

But what was I to do for money? Eventually, because we had so little in the way of income, the car my friend and I bought was repossessed and the phone was disconnected. I had no car or phone for nearly a decade. Thankfully, neighbors would take messages on occasion and give me a ride into town, where I had to amuse myself for their entire workday before catching a ride back to my country church.

I acquired a couple of weaving looms and proceeded to make fabric, scarves, ponchos, placemats, simple jackets. I tried to sell these items at the craft fairs that had begun to spring up in communities around me. People praised the work but rarely bought anything. I knew nothing about marketing, only wanted to make lovely things. I figured if I did a good job as a weaver, the things would sell themselves. Well, no...

Instead of moving on to some other project to earn money, I returned to rebel mode and wove pieces more challenging, much more technically challenging, to prove that I was good at this skill, to prove to myself that I was worthy. If twenty threads per inch was standard, I'd weave with thirty-six. If that seemed easy, then I'd weave silk satin at ninety threads per inch. I wove a large textured wall hanging using only shades of white (there are thousands). I was commissioned to weave a full-length cloak in colors to represent the Prairies. Although such projects never resulted in more sales, they did garner some financial support from Saskatchewan Arts Board grants and a gallery show or two.

Eventually, I received a Canada Council grant to weave ninety-threads-to-the-inch silk satin kimonos, with warps I painted with an airbrush. Weaving was a way to create order as well as beauty. A fifty-five-inch-wide silk warp of ninety threads per inch was more "order" than even I could imagine. It was so beautiful to thread onto the loom, so luscious to weave a fabric like this. It brought me more than just order—it brought me joy.

My days were filled with weaving and writing. One creates a lot of textile projects and writes a lot of words over the course of two decades. It was an amazingly productive time, and exactly what I needed to come to terms with my pain, and to make from it both beauty and the person I wanted to be.

And who did I want to be? Someone who knew who she was and could live comfortably in her own skin. Someone who did not take every possible opportunity to escape from herself into dissociation and numbness. Someone who felt it was safe to be alive, to walk down a street, to talk to people. Someone who didn't spend all her energy being afraid of everything. Someone who did not need to be so bloody hyperalert all the time.

As I approached forty, I still hadn't written about my experiences in a way that felt true and potent enough to convey how it really felt. I became ever more frustrated. I was writing so much that seemed useless, pointless, like it was never going anywhere. How could I change that? How would all this scribbling ever become something?

Then I had a health scare, and that certainly focused my mind. The doctor said, *Tumor, possible cancer.* I said, *Dammit, now or maybe never.* So I wrote a book, after thirteen years of apprenticeship and many efforts that went nowhere.

Writing a book does not magically heal the wounds of a traumatized childhood and adolescence. When the book went out into the world, and I went with it, I suddenly had to talk more about my past than I'd ever imagined I would be required to do. And it made no sense to be a basket case in public. I'd have to fake it until I made it. I felt an obligation to my readers to have it mostly together, believing that I was given an opportunity to speak to other survivors about the possibility of healing. I felt I was more credible if I at least appeared to be on a healing path myself.

What I didn't appreciate until many years later was just how strong I had become after two decades of writing my way through and creating beautiful things. I went from hermit to public speaker in a heartbeat. Constantly traveling to conferences, events, readings from coast to coast in Canada and then in Europe for seven amazing weeks. I truly didn't have a clue I could do this ... the quaking, frightened little five-year-old I was convinced I still was inside at nearly forty.

I had eventually rewritten the narrative of my self, moving at a glacial pace from victim to survivor. It wasn't until I was on the road with my first book that I could see that I had survived. How would I have been able to do this constant touring and speaking for two years about the horror of what is done to children if I was not a survivor? How else could I listen to stories of abuse, each more horrific than the last, sometimes many dozen in an evening? How else could I stay present and engaged? How else could I be supportive to the women who trusted me to understand what they shared?

Each of us can do something positive with our profound learning and hard-won skills as survivors. We can become a beacon for the wounded around us. Sometimes all it takes is eye contact, a smile, a simple acknowledgment. Often what is required is that we be engaged, caring, and compassionate, sharing our stories and our truth. Silence has never done us any good. I had worked hard for twenty years, learning about and growing into my strength.

FOR THE WORK I needed to do I needed to be alone. We are not encouraged in our culture to spend time alone, thinking. Better to keep busy, surround yourself with people, events, parties. Just keep going, no matter how broken you feel. Push on through; it will be all right if you just keep busy. Have a baby, or another one—just keep busy. All that thinking is bad for you. Here, take this pill, and that one—just keep going. Of course, you need a relationship, any relationship; the bad boys will keep you from thinking about anything except how to manage them and yourself. Just carry on. No profit in thinking too much about it all. Do things for other people; never take care of yourself—that's selfish, and you cannot bear to be thought of as selfish. Empty yourself entirely; use all your energy for others. Surround yourself with drama—that will keep you from thinking. Then crash, burn out, and fall deathly ill.

The other option, the one I chose after trying most of the others, was to retire from the fray, to find a safe place to be alone. Aloneness comes with its own risks, of course, but I had a lifeline in place, a friend who believed in what I was trying to do and had promised to support me through the process. I had to hope that would be enough.

No one ever really knows how a decision made under duress will turn out. But I had a strange faith that this would work out okay. Even though there was rather a lot on the wrong side of the ledger: no money; no windows, heating, or plumbing in the church. But still, it was my lovely safe place, and somehow it would be okay. At the very least, I had the peace I needed to create beautiful things, write, and read.

I read everything I could find, everything by and about women. How did they survive in different eras? What did they do to create beauty, to make space to write, to raise their children, when there seemed no way to do these things? What were the backstories of famous women, what life experiences did they endure and survive? Virginia Woolf's *A Room of One's Own* was an ongoing inspiration. And the memoirs of May Sarton taught me more about solitude.

I read all the great feminist writers of the era: Betty Friedan, Germaine Greer, Alice Walker, Andrea Dworkin, Margaret Laurence, Marilyn French, Sylvia Plath, Doris Lessing, Starhawk, Marge Piercy, and Adrienne Rich. I read the feminist scholars who were rethinking and reconstructing the truth about women's lives and loves, history and language. Each book I read connected me to a half dozen others, and so it went for more than two decades.

Fiction, poetry, and scholarly works were all on the menu. I read about the early Christians because I wanted to know when and how women were written out of history. I read about archaeological digs that seemed to show that the erasure of women from the historical record is many millennia old. And even when modern archaeological projects turned up the so-called anomalies—artifacts that indicated that women were revered in the past as goddesses, bringers of life—those artifacts were dismissed as irrelevant. What apparently is relevant, always, are the artifacts of patriarchal male culture: weapons, fortifications, conspicuous wealth.

I also read to try to understand power: who has it, how it is used and abused, and who does not have it. Throughout recorded history, with very few exceptions, power has belonged to men of great wealth and social status. Women birthed and raised the children, provided the food, looked after the home, and men jostled for wealth and glory. Women were supposed to be the busy hens, men the strutting peacocks.

Nice work if you can get it, I suppose. What I still don't understand, after all these years, and all this thinking and reading, is why we women haven't done more to rebel against this world view and oppression. I'm certain I'm not the only female who attempted to rebel as a child. It couldn't go on this way if we seriously rebelled, all of us together. Sure, the occasional strike, march, or withdrawal of services sends a message to the current generation, but it doesn't change the overall power imbalance in our lives.

Economically, we barely seem to count—our work, from childbirth to emotional labor, is not valued the same as men's work. Our labors have been deemed insignificant. Men's labors are important, vital even, though they do not give life to much more than figures in some virtual ledger. And now the patriarchal mind-set is utterly destroying the planet, our beautiful blue orb, our mother ship, all in the name of those virtual figures. Patriarchy and toxic masculinity do not work for most men, or for women, children, and the planet.

I see my own experiences as a survivor of childhood sexual abuse and exploitation as part of a long patriarchal continuum: men start by raping and exploiting children, move on to raping and exploiting women, and end up raping and exploiting the earth. Men, and some women, protect other men they know are abusing children and women. So many people (both men and women) in my community knew what was going on, yet no one intervened. I found this incredibly shocking, having assumed what I endured was secret. There is a perception that if one criticizes male privilege and behavior, one either hates men or will suffer nasty consequences.

Solitude and, yes, hiding meant that I was reasonably safe from nasty consequences, other than poverty. Nasty consequences such as being declared insane and drugged into compliance with social norms, or as I had been previously threatened, being locked up.

MY HEALING PROJECT is a lifelong one. Over the last four decades, I have addressed as many of my hurts as I could and either reframed them or supplied the balm that would make me feel better and less wounded.

Then: I was always cold. There were never enough blankets or warm clothes, and one winter there was no heat. A Saskatchewan winter without heat—that's serious cold.

Now: I knit constantly: warm things for myself and presents for my friends. I have very toasty blankets, one of them handwoven, and a wool duvet. There is a wood stove in my sitting room.

Then: Hunger was a constant. There was rarely enough food to go around for ten children and little in the way of protein or vegetables.

Now: I cook and eat to my heart's content—and ever-expanding girth.

Then: *Tell me a story.* My exhausted mother never had time for this, and there were no books in the house.

Now: I have an extensive personal library and adore listening to audiobooks.

Then: I wanted to play the piano. But I was told I didn't deserve to, and besides, there was too much work for me to do.

Now: I will listen to anything by Bach for cello or piano. Classical, vocal, opera, ancient music, music on original instruments, chamber music, folk music—all nourish my spirit.

Happiness is found in the little things: A late-blooming rose in October. The first snowdrops poking through the earth in spring. I find my happiness in being able to look at my life and state: *I am where and who and how I want to be.* My plan is to be happy and to be generous with it, and to be grateful for what I have learned along the way. Not grateful for the suffering and misery but for the strength, courage, and wit to learn from my experiences and carry on. I'm grateful to be alive and not embittered, which is surely a miracle considering all the struggles I've endured. Grateful that I have learned to trust a little, often a qualified trust, but trust, even so. Grateful, too, that I am sane, and not overtly bent on self-destruction anymore. I am grateful to have arrived safely at an age I never imagined I'd achieve. I take joy in every day.

Some hurts may not heal. I can still be triggered, though not as often or easily as I once was. Now I have learned to recognize what's happening and calm myself down. I remind myself that I am okay now, that I am not in danger. If life presents me with an opportunity for healing, I take it. Just because a decade or six has passed doesn't mean there are not still options for healing.

At seventy, I face new challenges, and some of them open old wounds. Sexism, and now ageism, continues to affect my life. I live on a pension that still puts me below the poverty line, even though it is more money in a month than I've ever had before.

All I rebel against now is in my head, yet rebellion still seems to be a lifestyle. *No, I don't have to do the dishes*, says the ten-year-old rebel who still takes up space in my head. I did enough dishes as a kid to last several lifetimes—three times a day for twelve people, and no singing while I did them, not even hymns. I don't handle kitchen cleanup well (some friends would call this an understatement), though I have developed a much better relationship with food and nourishing myself, and I enjoy cooking more than ever. It is, of course, no safer to rebel as an older woman than it was as a young one. Now my concerns can be dismissed because as an older woman I am invisible and considered insignificant. That is particularly frightening when dealing with the medical establishment.

I no longer weave, but my current love affair with fiber has me knitting or spinning to create my own yarn every day, many hours a day. My project list is so extensive I will need another thirty or forty years to complete it. I am no slouch in the yarn and fleece stash department. Working with my hands, creating something beautiful and useful, has been and still is a vital part of my healing journey. The sheer joy these activities bring to my days cannot be overstated. I couldn't do without them.

I have always been extremely fortunate in my friends. These days, I enjoy the company of fiber friends, a group of marvelous women I call my tribe. I cherish them and know that I am cherished in return. I still prefer to spend a great deal of time in solitude, though it is now much more pleasant to be around people than previously. I am no longer alone if I don't wish to be.

For me, survival has required multiple strategies: solitude, fiber and artwork, writing and reading, and, importantly, learning to nurture and care for myself. Thus, I have created a decent life.

And, yes, the rage is still there too, when I need it.

SILENCE

·

Gwen Benaway

•

Wovon man nicht sprechen kann,
darüber muss man schweigen.

What we cannot speak about we
must pass over in silence.

—LUDWIG WITTGENSTEIN

WANT TO WRITE about the sky, and lakes underneath starlight. I want to write of possibility and newness, the way his skin tastes like the sun and dirt. I want to write about being holy. I never wanted to be a survivor, a girl who writes about trauma.

Do you know what it sounds like when a heron lifts off from a lake? It sounds like nothing. They are so powerful in their wings, so steady in their bodies, that they transition from one world to another without making a noise.

I want to be a heron.

I AM TALKING on the phone with my friend. She is another Indigenous trans girl. She just let a boy fuck her without a condom. He came inside her in the apartment he shares with his cis girlfriend. She says she didn't say yes to it, but she didn't say no. Imperfect consent. She tells me that a part of her wanted him to cum in her. An intimacy, a small claiming of bodies and love.

The cis girlfriend doesn't know about my friend, doesn't know her boyfriend is ejaculating inside a trans girl. My friend asks if she fucked up, if it's wrong to let a boy cum in you. Does she owe anything to the other girl? She went through the cis girl's things when he was in the shower. She tells me he says he loves her. She won't admit to me that she loves him, but I know anyway. I don't know how to answer her, so I say it's natural to want this form of intimacy with a boy you love. I validate her wanting.

She says he drove her home afterward, like this redeems him. I say that he must love her, because I know it's what she wants to hear. It's what I would want to hear. We fall silent for a moment. Her voice follows me into sleep that night. I dream of boys I've loved, their texts cascading around my body, and of trees moving in the night breeze.

TRANS GIRLS EXPERIENCE a unique form of misogyny, a violent intersection of being a woman and being trans. Like cis women, we are vulnerable to sexual assault, domestic abuse, catcalling, sexual harassment, and the thousand little ways that women's bodies are policed. Most of my trans girl friends have been sexually assaulted. But there are very few resources for trans women who have been raped.

Most rape crisis centers or supports are only for cis women. All women are vulnerable to rape, but girls like me face a heightened threat with dramatically fewer services for after-care. Being a trans girl in the world constitutes a trauma. Every part of our lives is saturated with violence. It's silent and insidious. We just live through, only talking about what happened when we are in rooms of other trans women.

What I envy in cis women is not their bodies but their possibility. Although cis girls share the same risks for violence as we do, I can't help but see that they also possess radically different opportunities for love and healing than we do. This is how privilege works, quietly offering up possibilities that pass by people with less of it. Isn't cis another word for privilege?

I remember listening to my ex-partner and his bro friends talking about girls in our living room. They went through a list of cis girls they knew, listing off their positive attributes. They gave one guy advice for seducing a cis girl, as if she were a prize fish to reel in. They agreed she would make a great girlfriend. Then one of the guys started talking about trans girls, how he was hanging around a local trans girl bar and chatting with one of the servers. "She's trans," he said, "but I think I might let her suck me off." Everyone laughed, so he added, "Well, it will make a good story!"

Another one of my Indigenous trans girl friends passes for cis. Like me, she is a preoperation trans girl who primarily dates men, but unlike me, she does not disclose being trans to them. She goes on dates, leads up to the moment of first sexual contact, and then does a trans reveal by dropping her panties in front of them. This is one of the most dangerous things that a trans girl can do. We are regularly murdered by cis male sexual partners. The term "trans panic"—cis men's sudden violent fear and repulsion in response to our bodies during sexual intimacy—has been used successfully in the US as a legal defense for murdering us.

When she told me about her nondisclosure approach, my immediate response was to condemn it. I told her she was going to get killed. She looked at me and shrugged before saying, "I don't like telling them I'm trans. They treat me differently if I do." I asked what she meant. "Well, they are really sweet and flirty before they know. Once I tell them, it's either all about sex, or they just want to be friends." Here is trans womanhood in motion, risking our lives to feel romance for a moment.

I hold another moment inside me. My ex-partner of five years was diagnosed with schizophrenia at the start of our romance. I spent a year helping him manage his medications and therapy appointments, comforting him when his moods plummeted. His doctor was weaning him off his medications, believing his psychotic episode was a result of his ADHD medications and not an underlying mental health condition. My ex was happy to go off his medications, even though it meant his sister and I had to watch for any signs of relapse.

We had just fucked. He turned to me and said, "Since I'm not crazy anymore, maybe I'll go back to dating regular girls." As if my love was only valuable when he felt unworthy of cis women's love. Another time after fucking, he told me how much better vaginal sex felt than anal sex, praising a pleasure I couldn't give him. I remember lying beside him, unable to sleep, feeling a hurt inside me that I've never healed.

This intersection of transness and misogyny is why I lied to my friend on the phone about the boy who came in her without asking. Both of us knew I was lying when I said he must love her. It's not like my friend hasn't been in this situation before, caught between a cis boy and a cis girl. Most straight trans girls have been in this situation. We know how it ends. He chooses the cis girl while we bundle our feelings into a tight knot in our hearts.

I could have told her that it's a form of sexual violence, him cumming in her without asking, that it's sexual violence against the cis girl as well. I could have confirmed what she already felt. Imperfect consent is imperfect violence. I didn't say any of these things. I told her to keep seeing him. Any love is better than no love, right?

I spend my days after our phone call regretting my words, twisting around my own memories of sexual violence and how I've internalized transmisogyny like a tree growing around a metal signpost. I can't sleep at night and spend the early-morning hours scrolling through cis girls on Instagram, tracking their likes, vacation photos, partner selfies, and nude shots. All I feel is how possible they are, how impossible I am.

I have no words for this feeling, but it is a dark thread inside me. It pulls me toward a violence I don't want but feel constantly. I am no different than my trans girl friends. I risk my body for love. I lie to myself. I tell myself he loves me when I know he doesn't. I pretend it's possible for me to experience positive sexual intimacy when I know it won't find me. Trans girls don't have the luxury of everyday romance.

I smoke on my balcony at 4 AM and think of my trans girl friends. I assuage my guilt and worry by praying, repeating a wordless prayer song I learned from my elder. The song moves around me like water. I hold an image of my friend in my mind, already awake and booking her appointment to get tested for HIV and other STIs. I send my prayer out to her, imagine it wrapping her bones in the love she deserves.

I whisper the words "*wintomoshiin mishomisinaank*" into the departing curls of gray smoke. Help us, ancestors.

Nothing answers me back. Silence swallows my prayers and our bodies. Trans girl prayers are as quiet as our graves.

I HAD A sex reassignment surgery (SRS) consult last week. It's what I have to go through to secure funding for my vagina. I have my second appointment this week. I cried after the first appointment, horrified by the images on the computer screen. The nurse forced me to watch a video of the surgery, images of a penis being severed and peeled into its soft tissue. I imagine she believed this was informed consent, but it felt like torture. I told my trans girl friends. They were horrified and offered to come to my second appointment. I said thank you, but I will not ask them to come with me.

What I don't tell anyone is I don't want to have the surgery. I do not want to experience the pain of the operation. My friend had it last month. She described the pain like a constant headache in the bottom half of her body. Her doctor increased her opioids to counter the pain, but she said it just made it bearable. She had a complication in the middle of the night. An abscess formed in her labia and burst. Blood ran down her legs and covered the ambulance floor. The doctor at the hospital fixed it, but all I can imagine is her at midnight, bleeding and crying with strangers.

Her boyfriend was with her throughout the operation and recovery. I don't have a boyfriend. It's too late now, less than five months out from my likely surgery date. Even if I met someone, there isn't enough time to bond enough to survive what my surgery would mean. One of my closest friends offers to go with me, a trans girl who has decided not to get the surgery. I am grateful but doubtful. Friendships are fragile. They break and change like ice floes on the river.

I do not want to be alone. Waking up in pain, alone in the recovery room, unable to walk for three days, a catheter between my legs. My friend said there was so much blood after her surgery that the nurses changed her sheets every six hours. Her boyfriend held her hand while she cried during dilation. Who will hold my hand?

The nurse made me write a four-page letter for the surgeon's office explaining my reasons and naming who will support me while I recover. The letter blinked at me from her computer screen. She made me watch as she filled in the template, parsing out my life into a paragraph. Ms. Gwen. Trans woman. Hormone replacement therapy for one year. Lived socially as a woman for a year and four months. I said I was a nonsmoker. She kept asking me if I have ever had any mental health issues. When I said no, I could see doubt on her face, but we kept going.

I lied to the nurse. I like my body as it is. I enjoy the complications of it, the possibilities. How it possesses the ability to be many things, to fuck and be fucked, and give head and receive head. How I am straight and queer, a woman who is not easy to define. I like the hardness between my legs meeting the softness of my body. How my breasts look in the mirror after I shower, two soft points along a lean line that runs toward a small cock. This body, this beautiful body I've made through hormones and prayers.

The problem is not my love of my body, but the desire of men. How a boy came into my life, held my hand on dates, and drove me home. His mouth on my mouth, his arms around me. Then rupture, telling me he didn't want a relationship. He said it wasn't because I was trans. Three weeks after he broke up with me, he started dating a cis girl. I am not supposed to internalize this as violence, just the realities of intimate love, but it feels like violence.

I don't want to have a conversation about my genitals. I don't want to hear another boy tell me they are curious, or they are not sure if they will get hard with me. I watch them flirt with cis girls, an easy nervous flutter in their eyes as they woo and dart around them. I feel an ache in my body. They look at me with fear or restraint. Careful of the transsexual, her touch and her body and her love.

I didn't say any of this to the nurse while she evaluated my readiness for surgery. I will never say any of this. I talk to my friends about the surgery, but I don't say why I am doing it. I rode in a car with two of my friends the day afterward, talking about social justice and being trans. We checked out my ex-boyfriend on Instagram. We found his new girlfriend and liked some of her photos. Trans girls being dangerous. I laughed with them. We played a French punk girl band on the car's speakers.

When I got home, I cried in my bed. The next day, I hid out in a park and imagined myself with a vagina. I felt grief about what I will destroy in my body, how I will bend it toward their love with blood and pain. An offering, my flesh and suffering for their desire. I know this is wrong, so I don't say it aloud, even to myself.

Will having a vagina heal me? No, it won't. Will it make me a cis girl? No, nothing ever can. Will boys finally see me as real? Maybe. Do I love my body more than I love them? I guess not.

Silence is the only way I can hold this violence.

I USED TO write about being trans all the time. I had a blog when I first transitioned. I was convinced that writing would save me. If I wrote about trans girl sex and love, boys would realize it's okay to desire us. To fuck and date us. I pretended this was for all of us as trans women, but if I'm honest, it was always about me.

Nothing changed from my writing. People consumed it. Thousands of views per month. My poems shared on social media, published nationally. My voice on the radio, saying trans girls are worthy of love. The truth is, nothing I said or wrote fixed anything.

I can't render this body beautiful with language. Make myself desirable or human by naming how I'm erased by the politics of desire. I have this persistent urge to say to the boys I know that if I weren't trans, they'd fall in love with me. I am learning to keep my mouth shut. Some truths are larger than me. I can't speak them, no matter how blessed I am with language.

An older trans woman attacked me in conversation for how I write about being trans. She said she was worried about employment when she transitioned, whereas I seem to only care about my love life. As if my love life is a luxury of my body. As if exposing this to the world in poems and articles is an act of my narcissism.

I was at a poetry reading recently. A novice poet got up and read her work. She was nervous. Her husband watched and clapped loudly for her. Her poetry was not perfect, but it was honest. One of her lines struck me, and I keep repeating it in my head. She said a girl is always beautiful in the eyes of someone who loves her. I hold these words inside me like a prayer.

Is a trans girl only heard by the ears of someone who loves her? I don't want to convince boys that trans girls are sexy and lovable. I want that to be something they already know. My writing about our desirability is another kind of violence.

The most beautiful things I write are the spaces between my words.

I SPEND MUCH of my time with new poets talking about line breaks. The space between images in poetry is sacred. Where there is emptiness, there is possibility.

Do you know what the most beautiful part of a man's body is? The space between his ears and his head, the room between his tongue and his lips, the distance between his shoulder blades, and the span of his fingers in your hand. How his cock rises up from his body, delineating his desire into openness. The soft line behind his scrotum to his anus, where shadow falls on his body. When he touches you inside your openness.

This is line breaks in poetry. Or silence in life. How beauty lives in wide spaces. What I love about boys is the things they don't say. How their silence can constitute a greater love.

Line breaks, writing about trauma, being a survivor. I could explain this more, but I don't want to. Like my lovers, what I don't say means more than what I do.

I TALK TO my therapist about my childhood and when I was raped. He gives me advice on my relationships. He encourages me to relearn intimacy with the people in my life. I attend a trans girl support group. My therapist watches my interactions in a social setting and suggests small corrections. We meet once a week for an hour and a half. He knows more about me than anyone.

These conversations are threads running through my life. I think about things he has said to me when I'm hanging out with other people. I replay conversations in my mind after they've happened and decide what I should have said. The funny thing about being a survivor is learning how to have relationships from strangers you pay. Maybe it is working. I seem calmer, more open to the world than ever before. I imagine other possibilities for myself. Being in love and holding someone. Experiencing intimacy without being afraid.

But there is always a moment in our sessions when I stop talking. We fought about these silences in the beginning. He would jump in and push our conversation toward some deeper explanation. I would get angry, snap at him, until the session would fall apart. He asked me what I wanted from him when I stopped talking. I didn't know how to answer him, but after three fights, I asked him to tell me that it would be okay.

"I want you to comfort me," I said, fidgeting on the couch.

"It's hard to know what you want, Gwen," he answered. "You are one of the smartest clients I've ever had, and it's hard to imagine you wanting something so surface. It almost seems like an insult to say something like that to you."

My silence is an invitation to love me. No one hears that but me. I always hear it.

WRITING ABOUT THE moments that have broken me open does not sew me together. Being raped, my dad hitting me. The survivor revelation, the flashback scene on the television show. I am not going to write this. Perhaps you feel cheated by my silence. Maybe you are disappointed, but I am disappointed by my writing daily. By my failure to transform, to heal.

I do not want to write about being a survivor. It may help you, but it has never helped me. If we were sitting together in a room and you asked me to talk about my trauma, I would probably say some really profound shit about it. You would feel inspired and grow a thin streak of pity for me.

Then you would talk about something from your life and we'd bond over it. We would smoke and talk, and everything would temporarily feel better. Then you would go on with your life, and I would sit alone, light another cigarette, and stare into the silent distance.

This moment, the one you will never see or understand, is the real truth. I cannot give this to you. I am tired of trying to give it to you. It is mine until I die.

I HAVE WRITTEN three collections of poetry. I am writing a fourth collection in between work emails. If you Google me, you will find dozens of personal essays on being Indigenous and being trans. I am one of the most widely published trans girls in Canada. My work is taught in six universities across North America and anthologized internationally. I have performed for audiences of three hundred in professional theaters.

I have made a life from speaking about trauma and being a survivor. I have written poems about rape and child abuse. I have held the hands of other survivors after readings, told them I understand, and witnessed their pain. I have influenced and mentored other poets as they emerged their craft.

I am tired of writing about my trauma. It has not saved me. I used to think it could, but now I know better. There is more to life than your trauma. What I want is not another book of poetry or another magazine article. What I want is a miracle. I want to fall asleep beside another body, listen to the sound of breath moving through their body. I want to leave the city and eat ice cream in a park. I want to hold someone's hand.

Writing has not brought me any miracles. Someone told me I would be a famous poet someday. I wanted to reply how much more I want to be loved, but you don't say that to people. People assume being a writer is being powerful. Writing is the opposite. It is making yourself vulnerable to an audience who will read your work, comment how much it means to them, and then leave you.

Writing about trauma is being abandoned again. Writing is learning to live inside your failure to heal. Writing is naming every hope in your chest and watching them fly away to the skyline. Writing will not give me what I need.

So why do I continue to write? Because language is my first love. Like all great loves, you are hurt more by what it can't give than what it can.

I want to break up with writing. Go no contact. Stop naming the things that wound me. Nurture the quiet longing of my body. Give nothing to the world but what I want to. Return to my private silence.

I WANT TO go to a lake. I want to take my clothes off and slide into icy water. I want to move out to the edge of deep water, where I can barely feel the bottom. I want to float in that cold and moving expanse of water. I want to be wild in the waters of my ancestors. I want to be a body beneath a sky underneath a flat sheet of moisture. I want to smell the musk of lake water, silt, and possibility.

I want to disappear. I want to be a girl who disappears.

I want to go to a city by an ocean. I want to watch movies in the dark. I want to make French dinners. I want to return to your basement room beside Woodbine station. I want to be touched without hesitation. I want to have adventures and fall in love and take risks and ride a bicycle to the edge of the city.

I want to be silent. I want to never write or talk again.

I want. I have always wanted. This want is what wounds me. I want to be a different kind of girl. I want a different body, another set of genitals. I want to not want any other body than the one I have. I want my childhood to have never happened. I want to not be a survivor.

I want to pass this want to you in silence.

THE HAPPIEST MOMENT in my life was riding in a car with my ex-boyfriend and his parents. It was night in late December, just before Christmas. We were in Alberta, driving home from Banff in the quiet dark of his parents' car. His dad and mom in the front seat, his hand in mine. We did not speak. Just the sounds of the highway, the heater blowing through the vents, and our movement toward his childhood home.

I like this memory. It replays within me. Riding in the front seat of a boy's car, him driving me home after fucking me, as small and silent as I've ever been. A boy holding my hand, turning it over in his hand, squeezing with a gentleness in his eyes, a soft wonder around us. Smoking with my friends in a parking lot, each of us trans and each of us staring at the moon, saying nothing. Every moment silence has given me, when the ones I love have touched me without words. When I am whole, not explaining or answering or making something ugly sound pretty.

I have spent my entire life explaining myself to social workers, lovers, doctors, therapists, and readers. What if language has limits? Silence is the only way to hold the experiences of my life. I will keep writing, but sometimes, I want to be silent.

Silence is the only way a survivor can be loved. You don't know what I've lived through. I can never tell you. I don't want to tell you, to harm you with how I've been harmed. I will not give you what has been given to me.

I IMAGINE ANOTHER life for myself. In this life, I am a sweetness like honey and whiskey poured over brown sugar cubes. I am soft. I am held in the arms of a boy who smells like tree bark and old books. I move without hesitation. In this life, this life I will never touch, I am wild and free inside a body that knows nothing of surgery. Or rape. Or being beaten. I sing inside the bones I carry.

In this fantasy, I have moments of silence as well. The difference is in what the silence tells you. In this other body, this other girl I will never know, her silence is her love. It does not translate her pain but her wonder.

I dream of this silence like a lake dreams of the sky.

THE QUIET ICE

·

Karyn L. Freedman

●

I LIKE THE SOUND of quiet, but it is not the noise of the city that bothers me. It's the activity in my head, the piercing images and intrusive thoughts that took root in the summer of 1990, when I was raped at the age of twenty-two while backpacking through Europe, and that appear to be mine for life. Over the years, I have come to understand that the recurring din in my head is just one of the consequences of psychological trauma, of being held captive and rendered helpless in the face of a terrorizing life event. When that happens, our biological impulse to flee or fight is blocked, which invites a kind of disorder to settle into the body. Like all forms of anxiety, trauma can be an occupying force, and the trauma that laid claim to me close to three decades ago has been relentless. Ill equipped to deal with the violence of that summer night, I spent my twenties pretending that what had happened to me was no big deal. Awash with shame, I kept the story of my rape a secret, as if not talking about it would make it go away, but my body has always known better. For years my nervous system was caught in an elevated state of arousal, easily startled, just waiting for the next catastrophe. After nearly a decade of struggling in silence I had had enough, and as I entered my thirties I decided to face the aftermath of my rape. I began to see a therapist, a privilege that has been my saving grace. But it was a decision that I made some years later, in September 2005, when I was thirty-seven years old, that helped me find the elusive sound of quiet in my head. That fall I joined a women's hockey league.

IT IS JUST after 4 PM on a Saturday and I've got an early game tonight, which means that I have only one more hour to kill before it's time to leave my house for the rink across town. It hasn't been a great afternoon, following a crappy night. I went to bed early, tired from a busy day of work. I poured myself some Scotch and read for a bit before turning out the lights, but two long hours of listening to my own heartbeat later, I flipped the lights back on. That woke up my partner, who stumbled out of bed and headed, half-awake, for the guest bedroom. Watching him leave, I resigned myself to the fact that it was going to be one of those nights. I sat up and took a pill for anxiety. While I waited for that to kick in, I poured some more Scotch, picked up my book, and began all over again. As a result, my head hurts and my chest has been tight all day. But none of that will matter soon. I decide to get to the game a bit early. While the others trickle in, I unzip my hockey bag and begin the ritual of putting on my gear. The room fills up and gets louder, everybody happy to be there and looking forward to the game. Already I am feeling better, and by the time I take my first warm-up lap around the rink, the distractions of the day have all but disappeared. I am gliding effortlessly through a refreshing, cool breeze, and as I round the corners all I can hear is the glorious grinding sound of my skate blades biting the ice. It's just about time to play.

I GREW UP in Winnipeg, which is the geographical center of Canada, and which can sometimes feel exactly like the middle of nowhere. The summers are beautiful but short, and the protracted, cold winters would be even harder were it not for the expansive prairie sun reflecting off the snow-covered city. Here, for a lot of people, hockey is a way of life. Professional hockey came to Winnipeg in the early 1970s with the Jets, a founding franchise in the World Hockey Association. But if ripples of excitement reverberated throughout the city in 1972 over the multimillion-dollar signing of Bobby Hull—the Golden Jet—they weren't felt at our dinner table. I was the middle of three girls, and I can assure you that not one of us spent our Saturday nights watching *Hockey Night in Canada*. My parents had no particular interest in winter sports, and hockey was not one of the extracurricular activities at Ramah Hebrew School, a private school that I attended from Grade 1 to 6. As a kid, I took swimming lessons, gymnastics, and, for a minute, piano, but I didn't see a pair of skates until I attended River Heights Junior High. Public school was an exciting new world, full of enticing opportunities for adventure. I made new friends and began to experiment with some of the finest homegrown Manitoba weed of the day. River Heights was a predominantly white, middle-class neighborhood, and most of the boys I met in junior high had grown up playing hockey—only boys, of course. Although pioneering women in Canada had been playing hockey for close to a hundred years, this was the early eighties and, as a rule, girls didn't play the game. Girls played ringette, which is also a team sport played with sticks on ice, but players must spear a ring with a bladeless stick and pass it across blue lines down the ice before trying to score. In Grade 8, my friends and I decided to sign up for the ringette team at our local community center. We were called the River Heights Snowbirds, and it was my first time on skates. It wasn't hockey, but at the time I didn't know any better, and I loved it. I had an oversized faded blue Snowbirds hoodie that I never took off. If I recall correctly, there was only one person on our team, a girl named Tracey, who actually knew how to skate. Although I was new to the game, I was completely and obliviously fearless, hurtling myself around the rink. It was absolutely thrilling. I spent more time on my butt than on my feet, and I played for only one year, but it was a beginning.

I DIDN'T THINK about hockey again until Grade 11, when I happened to fall in love with a hockey player. We were both students at Kelvin High School, but neither of us attended very many classes. He was too busy with hockey, which would eventually take him to a long career in the National Hockey League, while I was continuing my experimentation with Manitoba's hydroponic best. I didn't care much about hockey, but I was crazy about him. And although

I wasn't looking for a role model, I could have done a lot worse. He was a gritty player with plenty of character, the kind who leads his team on and off the ice. I quickly grew accustomed to the cold hard benches and lukewarm hot chocolate that typified arenas around town, and in spite of myself, I began to learn something about the game. That knowledge stuck with me, even though hockey fell off my radar after we broke up.

AFTER HIGH SCHOOL graduation, I moved to New York City to go to school, but after a couple of years I returned home to take philosophy at the University of Manitoba. I was happy to be studying philosophy and not unhappy to be back in Winnipeg, and I had big summer plans. I was going overseas for the first time to spend a couple of months backpacking through Europe. I began my trip in Israel and then visited a dozen or so European cities, each more interesting and charming than the last, from Prague to Rome to Budapest to Berlin. It was an intoxicating time, but the airy, warm excitement of summer came to an abrupt end on the night of August 1, 1990, in a high-rise apartment on Boulevard Masséna in the thirteenth arrondissement of Paris. The tenth-floor apartment was being rented by the poet and literary critic Édouard Roditi, and when I arrived there earlier that day, Roditi had two houseguests staying with him. One was an ex-boyfriend of mine from New York, a student of Roditi's at Bard College. The other was a thirty-year-old Frenchman, a big guy with dark hair and kind of bad skin, who, I later learned, had spent half of his adult life in jail for petty crimes. His name was Robert (*row-bear*)

Dinges. He seemed friendly enough, and I didn't think twice about being left alone with him in the apartment when my ex headed out the door to meet Roditi for dinner. Robert kindly offered to make me some food, and then afterward, pressing a long sharp knife against my neck with one hand and firmly gripping my short hair with the other, he raped me multiple times in multiple ways before taking me from the apartment, still at knifepoint, while threatening to kill me. From the moment that knife first grazed my neck until I broke free of Robert's stranglehold in the lobby of the apartment building one hour later, I was rendered mute, jammed in a state of sheer terror that later imploded in my body and stayed lodged there for decades.

ROBERT BOLTED OUT the building's main door after I broke free. The police arrived within minutes of my escape, called by a man who had been in the lobby and who had understood, through my uncontrollable sobbing and broken French, that something very bad had just occurred. They asked me a couple of quick questions, and then a number of them took off in search of Robert, while I went with the others to the local police station to give a detailed statement of the crime. By then I had moved from a kind of scattered hysteria to a pulsating shock. I was desperate to call home and experienced a surge of relief when I finally spoke to my parents, who immediately began working with the Canadian Embassy in Paris to get me on the next plane back to Winnipeg. In the meantime, I was taken to a hospital to get checked out and have a rape kit done. Then I was deposited back at the police station, where I bided my time until I could fly home the next day. I arrived in Winnipeg in much the same condition that I left Paris—which is to say, totally wired. The trauma of the night before was already working its way through me, but I had absolutely no idea how to deal with that, so I ignored it as best I could and contorted back into my life. I returned to school in the fall and tried to keep busy, pushing my way through flashbacks and sleepless nights. There was the odd interruption from Paris along the way: first, when Robert was found and arrested, and then, some months after that, when he tested HIV positive. I also had to return to Paris a couple of times in those first couple of years: initially to give testimony at Robert's pretrial hearing, and then later for the trial, whereupon he was sentenced to eight years in jail. But I buried whatever distress those barbed reminders of Boulevard Masséna caused me alongside the events of the night of August 1, 1990. I just wanted to forget about it all and get on with my life. I finished one degree and started on the next, while working my way through one fraught relationship and then another. And somewhere along the way, in the midst of all of that, I rediscovered the game of hockey.

IT HAPPENED ALMOST by chance. From 1993 to 1996, I lived with a boyfriend in a large two-bedroom apartment on the second floor of a house that was tucked in a back lane behind a pharmacy on Sherbrook Street, just south of Winnipeg's downtown core. We had a big television in the second bedroom, which we used as a den, where we spent countless winter nights drinking beer and watching hockey with our pals. Initially, I joined in happy for the distraction, but before long I found myself tuning in in earnest. The bits and pieces of the game that I had picked up from my high school sweetheart were rounded out, and soon enough I was following along with a kind of fervor that took me by surprise. Now I had my favorite players, coaches, broadcasters, and even referees, as well as opinions on every aspect of the game. I kept up with the relevant stats and woke up each day to watch highlights from the previous night. I had become a certified fan, and the Winnipeg Jets were my team. They have never been a great team, the Jets, not before they crushed the hearts and souls of Winnipeggers by moving to Phoenix in 1996, and not since returning to Winnipeg in 2011. However, for a few years in the early nineties, there was some cause for hope. This was a team that was exciting to watch. Teemu Selänne—the Finnish Flash—scored seventy-six goals in his remarkable first season, which is still the league record for the most goals by a rookie in a season. Teemu and the team's other stars were supported by a stable of solid players, not necessarily big point-getters but the kind of players who earned their places in the lineup every night. Goaltending had been a perennial problem for the Jets, but in January 1995, they started Russian goalie Nikolai Khabibulin. When he first arrived in Winnipeg, he didn't speak a word of English, but that was no obstacle for the Bulin Wall, who was spectacular in net. He was thrilling to watch, even if he was inconsistent. His entertaining style was never more on display than in the Jets' first-round playoff series against the Detroit Red Wings in April 1996, their last hurrah before leaving for Phoenix. The Jets were down in the best-of-seven series by three to one when the series returned to Joe Louis Arena in Detroit for Game 5. No one expected the Jets to beat the Red Wings at home, but with more than just the series on the line, Khabibulin put on a joyous demonstration of hockey artistry, stopping fifty-one of fifty-two shots and giving the Jets a win—and a chance to come home for at least one more game. The Jets returned home to lose Game 6 and the series, and the city lost its team, but at least the fans got to say a proper good-bye. I was leaving, too. That fall, I moved to Toronto to go to school—and swapped the interminable anguish of loving one losing team for loving another.

THE TRAUMA THAT results from terrifying life events over which we have no control is profound. It changes us in fundamental ways. The paralyzing helplessness of being trapped in a threatening situation results in a severe disruption of the nervous system. This extreme stress affects how the brain works and makes it difficult for survivors of traumatic events to regulate their everyday biological functions—sleeping, breathing, talking, even eating. Psychologically traumatic experiences are harmful to the body in ways that are belied by the fact that in some instances we can escape these events with no physical wounds. I had spent the better part of a decade bracing for what was coming next as the trauma that had taken root within me expanded into a crushing anxiety that ultimately became impossible to ignore. My body, it seemed, was no longer my own, its recalcitrant movements reflexively attuned to events of the past. This was never more conspicuous than when I was having sex. The notion that rape is about power and not sex is misleading. It is true that people who rape often do so to exert power over their victims, but for rape survivors, whose bodies have been used sexually without their consent, the transgression can live on in their sex lives. At least, that's what happened to me. Sex had become a series of triggers that prevented me from intimacy, my inhospitable body populated by land mines sensitive to the touch. This situation became particularly acute as I entered a new relationship in my early thirties. Prior to that I had been able to have sex and occasionally even enjoy it, but now every caress threw me back to an unwanted memory. I struggled through a trial of panic attacks while attempting to ignore the suffocating memory of my rapist's sweaty flesh draped on top of me, behind me, in front of me. I couldn't breathe. These images colonized my thoughts and kept me up at night. I began to lean on alcohol to trick my body into relaxing, but that was its own trial. And besides, the unwanted images returned in my dreams. At some point, I broke. Unable to move forward, I decided it was time to get help. With financial backing from my parents, I sought out a therapist and began the long process of healing.

THE CHANCE TO work on my own recovery has been one of the great privileges of my life, and I was lucky to find an exceptional therapist. She helped me to see the far-reaching influence of traumatic experiences. With the benefit of her insight, I came to understand that in order to dull the force of the images in my head I had to first live in them.

Repressing them was not going to work, at least not for me, not in the long run. Traumatic memories stick with us, in one way or another, whether or not we invite them to do so. Facing them head on gave me a chance to deflate the power they had over me. In the safety of my therapist's office, I would close my eyes and return to Boulevard Masséna, only this time without the threat of the knife against my neck, though it didn't always feel that way. It was scary at first, but in time I allowed myself to remember that hour of terror in all its vividness, and to say and think and feel everything that I couldn't at the time. This was some of the hardest work I have ever done, but eventually, I started to feel lighter, freer. Not all at once, and not completely, but incrementally, here and there. But there remained times when my body felt sluggish and pinned down, as if Robert were still on top of me. In these moments, my legs were heavy and there was a constricting weight on my chest. It was as if certain elements of the trauma had remained inaccessible through traditional psychotherapy. Talking about feeling had taken me a long way, but because the trauma had settled in my body, it seemed that I needed to physically move about to thoroughly process it. I was desperate to shake my legs free and push Robert off of me. I needed to scream and punch and kick and shout and get rid of the lingering anger and pain. My therapist suggested we take our work to a local trauma resource center. It had sound-proof rooms, gym mats, and other props all geared to the idea that physical movement is essential to processing body memories. Here, with the lights dimmed, I would put on boxing gloves and try to move around. This was a new kind of hard, but at some point, I found my strength. And then, session after session, I pounded away at the unwanted images of that night, my movements finally under my command. Recovery is not a linear process, but I could feel myself moving forward, becoming less blocked. I had been given the chance to redefine my body, which was once again my own. There remained only one thing left for me to do.

THE FALL OF 2005 was not an easy time for me. I was a few years into a tenure-track job in philosophy at the University of Guelph, and I was feeling the pressure. Trauma is a chronic condition, so no matter how much work I did to heal from the events of that summer night in Paris, in times of high stress my body still responded as if it were under threat. My heart sped away from me as my trembling voice betrayed my inability to take a deep breath, the panic of the moment transparent. As I cycled through these familiar feelings, I realized that I needed something in addition to therapy to help get me through tough times. I had tried yoga, but it was too meditative for me. I was craving the kind of physical release that I had found at the trauma resource center, something fast-paced to counter the sluggishness in my legs. And then, one day, it just clicked. I was still watching hockey all the time, by this point a long-suffering Toronto Maple Leafs fan. So why wasn't I playing the game that I had loved for so long? I bought some equipment and signed up for a Saturday night women's league. That first year wasn't easy. I wasn't always comfortable getting changed in front of other people, a vulnerability made worse because I didn't know anyone on my team—or in the league, for that matter. Also, I was a real beginner. I knew the rules as well as anyone, but playing was different than watching. I was shaky on skates, and I couldn't make a good line change to save my life. Yet it was clear to me from the start that I was onto something. Although I wasn't any good, I worked hard, and that intense physical effort coupled with the sharp mental focus that the game demands helped dull the noise in my head. And the better I got, the more focused I became, and the more control I had over my body. I could not have predicted it, but playing hockey turned out to be the way to quiet the persistent images in my head. Playing hockey helped me become unstuck. And now, after many years of playing, it has become much more than that.

I AM SITTING on the bench, breathing heavily after my last shift, my face red hot with effort, watching the play as it goes up and down the ice, and anticipating the moment when I get to jump back into the game. Fortunately, we have a short bench tonight, so I know it won't be long. The time comes, and once again I am free. My body moves in sync with the game, and for the time being, there is nothing else in the world I care about. The sounds of the arena fade away and the quiet in my head returns as my focus narrows in on the play. I'm on left wing tonight, holding my position on my own blue line as the play moves dangerously around our net. Our goalie deflects a shot that lands deep in the corner behind her goal line, and my eyes are trained on my teammate who retrieves the puck and sends it up the boards, where I am waiting to receive it. The hard sound of it landing on my stick has me pivoting forward. I am thinking of nothing but moving the puck up the ice. I've got some room, so I begin to carry it through the neutral zone before passing it across the ice to an open winger, who successfully dumps it into the offensive zone. It is the right move, and the momentum is on our side. I chase down the play and regain control of the puck behind the other team's net. At that moment, time slows right down. Tonight, we're lucky. We're a bit faster than the other team, and that edge means I've got some time with the puck. For at least a few seconds, I can see the ice clearly. I spot an open player in front of the net. We lock eyes. I send the puck her way and watch it cut a clean line through a mess of skates and land on her stick. It's a good pass. It doesn't matter that we didn't score, and it doesn't matter that we didn't win the game. The unmitigated joy of being able to see that play, and then move the puck to where I know it ought to go, leaves me exhilarated and at peace.

FOR A LONG time, the search for stillness in this fast game was the main reason I played hockey. I am not a great player. I am not the fastest skater or the most skilled, and I will never possess the gracefulness of those women who grew up on skates. But I fight hard for the puck and I look to make the play. And then, of course, there is the rush of the game. The scraping of skates on hard ice and the surge of cool air that washes over you as you chase down the puck or fight for it in the corners. The divine feeling you get when you make a good pass or when you hear the almost inaudible whoosh as the puck you fired hits the back of the net. I now have three games a week in leagues and arenas all around town. Because I am on the ice a lot, I watch less hockey than I used to, and that's fine with me. Although I still live in Toronto, the Jets are again my team, and with the arrival of another Finnish superstar, they are finally looking good. Watching players of all skill levels move up and down the ice makes it clear to me that the release I get from playing is something many people experience. You do not need to have lived through a traumatic experience to find tranquility on the ice. And, for me, over the years, the game has become even more than that. I now belong to a glorious hockey community, one that is bursting with the most incredible women, women of all ages and sizes and occupations. It is an open and welcoming community, and I can't believe my good luck in finding it. But I try not to dwell on that. My worry is that if I get lost in a happy thought, I might miss an important clue, some signal that danger is just around the corner. In those moments, I begin to feel the familiar creep of that anxious dread and the expectation of catastrophe that comes with it, and the very images that I play the game to forget come back to me. I see myself losing an edge and crashing headfirst into the boards, or slamming hard against another player, or my legs twisting beneath me, a heap of broken bones, after a terrible fall, and I have to tell myself to breathe. When the panic returns, I am reminded that the experience of being raped has left me permanently wounded. I think back to that night in Paris, and I wonder how I could have missed the warning signs, how it was that I didn't see what was coming next.

I know I am not to blame for what happened to me, even if sometimes my body tells me otherwise.

The struggle between how I feel and what I know to be true is mine for life, but once I am back on the ice, all I care about is making the play, and the quiet in my head returns.

THIS (TRAUMATIZED, KINKY, QUEER) BODY HOLDS A STORY

•

Amber Dawn

•

Small-Town Southern Ontario, 1990

I am a poor, white, small-town slut and, uniquely, the small-town slut who cries while performing blow jobs. Sometimes, I hang out in the loading zone of our high school's woodshop and smoke cigarettes with other small-town sluts, who try to coach me on overcoming my gag reflex. We practice pinching our noses and inching our fingers into each other's mouths until we retch or burst out laughing. This scene could be one of the many possible origin stories of my queer and kinky identities, but more than anything, I just want to belong, to be a part of something. I like the sisterhood of being a small-town slut.

I still cry when there's a dick in my mouth. The sisterly deep-throat practice didn't solve the problem, as the cause is not limited to my uvula, soft palate, or tongue. Trauma inhabits the entire nervous system. I am a survivor of sexual abuse by multiple perpetrators. I am possessed by trauma, which began in early childhood and—though my sixteen-year-old self does not yet know it—will prevail through my twenties and early thirties, when I am both an outdoor/indoor sex worker and a creative writing student.

All of the teenage boys I bang openly admit that my tears make them uncomfortable. I am not bewildered by their openness; rather, it is their capacity to maintain rock-hard erections despite their discomfort that confuses me.

My on-again, off-again boyfriend suggests we do it to happy music: 10,000 Maniacs' *In My Tribe* album or anything by the Sugarcubes. He hopes the buoyant and unmistakable female vocals of Natalie Merchant or Björk will soothe me into happy, normal sex.

I present a counteroffer: I ask him to drag me down the shag-carpeted staircase in his parents' house and mount me beside the front door as I pretend to reach helplessly for the doorknob. This request gives him nightmares. It causes him to look over my shoulder and into the distance when he speaks to me. After a week or so without sex, however, he agrees, and I find myself screaming and spitting into the welcome mat at the entrance of his familial home.

What's wrong with these boys? How do they remain aroused when I am so clearly messed up, so traumatized? These are examples of time-wasting questions. I confess, I waste far too much time wondering what is wrong with men and boys. The real question—the question that benefits me—is what do men and boys and their rock-hard erections have to teach me? How are their desires and pleasures so undeterred by discomfort?

East Vancouver, 2017

I take a break from writing my novel to jerk off. A younger me might have controlled myself and stayed rooted firmly to my desk. Writing was serious and cerebral; masturbation was frivolous and vulgar. Or, that's not it—it's never been about vulgarity. I've been called vulgar before, along with whore, dyke, cunt, trash, freak, and other words I now regularly use to describe myself. I find that the bitterness of many pejoratives can be overturned and lovingly reclaimed. So, it's not the so-called vulgarity of jerking off that would have concerned a younger me. Younger me was burdened by a pejorative term I'd been newly introduced to in a creative writing workshop: confessional.

Confessional is what writers want to avoid, or so I was taught. Writing is not therapy or a status update. A writer must understand the difference between barfing their private lives onto the page and crafting the tragedies of humanity into capital *A* art. Write what you know, yes, but don't get "too personal" (almost always code for too far outside of the dominant narrative). Younger me most certainly heeded creative writing professors' warnings about being "too personal." Younger me nodded keenly as professors told me my memoir-in-progress "reads like fiction" and advised me to try writing in omniscient third person point of view. First person wasn't working; it made readers of my early work uncomfortable. Younger me switched my MFA thesis from memoir to fiction because my lived truths as a trauma survivor and queer sex worker simply fit better into a three-act structured narrative. Younger me followed this line of thinking until I arrived at the idea that all my writing must be intellectually divorced from my everyday experiential and embodied self. Younger me took up the sharp scalpel of craft and sliced into my life as if it were a long-dead cadaver, as if I no longer felt stories in my body.

Like other survivors, I am quite skilled at dissociation. I am used to my body—and all that it holds—being a non-priority. It was not, and is still not, hard for me to adopt this fractured sense of selves into my writing practice, or any other aspect of my life.

East Vancouver, 1998

Sex-positive, polyamorous twentysomethings bring spin-the-bottle parties back into fashion, and I am in the game. We're a circle of queers dressed in Canadian tuxedoes (denim on denim) or lingerie-as-outerwear. Most of us are whiskey-licked or coming up on MDMA. Each time the bottle stops, a new couple performs both derelict desire and shorthand negotiations of consent. "Tongue?" is a straightforward question, and, in this group, so is "Chokehold?"

My spin pairs me with a wiry butch I've never made out with before.

"Rough?" he asks.

"Rough," I agree.

"Spit?"

"Spit."

Our peers cheer as we yank one another around by the hair, licking and swapping spit.

Discovering my queerness reduces the amount of discomfort I shoulder as a promiscuous survivor. I don't rationally understand this at age twenty-four, not yet. But the feeling is there, the physical, fundamental feeling of my partners being okay with who I am. They don't maintain their rock-hard erections (corporeal or metaphorical) despite my roughness and trauma. My roughness and trauma *are* desirable.

Later that night, the wiry butch and I resume our make-out session in an empty warehouse loading zone a few blocks away from the party. We tease each other about the bruises we'll have in the morning. Our voices yelp and echo down the industrial alleyway. I think about how my expressions of pain were heavily moderated as a child; mine was a "Don't make a sound, or else" kind of abuse.

Don't think about being molested, I scold myself when he drops his pants, lets them fall down past his knees. I fuck him in the open night air with both hands.

He hooks his fervent thumbs into my underwear, says, "Let's get there together."

"No."

"No?"

I can't get to where this wiry butch is going. I suffer from physiological and cognitive symptoms of shame (like nausea and suicidal ideation) after orgasm. Again, at twenty-four, I don't rationally understand the many effects of trauma. What I know is my orgasm makes me sick.

At the height of the queer nineties, I've proven to be too boundaried, too cold compared to my slut-loving peers. What if I'll never be as empowered and reciprocating of a lover as sex-positivism encourages? But this question, too, is theoretical; it's abstract and academic. Shame-sickness is real. Gradually, I adopt a stone femme identity—a femme who won't let sex partners near her cunt. If I compartmentalize my cunt, maybe I can remain as slutty as I want to be. I render myself niche within a sexual movement that's already on the margins. I feel oppressively small, because I am.

Throughout my twenties, I see doctors who prescribe clozapine and Ambien. I join a support group for adult survivors of sexual abuse and never disclose that I'm queer and a sex worker. I pay an asinine amount of money for hypnotherapy sessions. I complete *The Courage to Heal* workbook. I write mock letters to my abusers. I write autobiographical poetry in the second or third person point of view. I convince myself that trying is the healing; therefore, I should try whatever is considered therapeutic. I am more adventurous with therapeutic practices than I am with sex. All of these therapeutic practices and coping, or being, strategies offer me varied comforts, yet none expunges the past from the present. No matter how I try, nothing separates; it remains.

South Surrey, 2004
The new girl and I stare through a two-way mirror into the massage parlor lobby. Crybaby sits neatly on the leopard-print sofa waiting for the new girl—his pick for the session—to escort him into a private room. I suggest she bring him to the blue room. The lighting is darkest in the blue room.

"He's a regular," I tell her. "He tips well, and he always cries at the end of his session."

"He looks so normal."

This girl is really new, I think, another young turn-out thrown into a hypersexualized environment without training or resources. Sex work is misogyny magnified. Women are male-gratification providers; that *is* the job. Women shoulder shame and stigma, which are perpetual by-products of the job (and of womanhood). Women are responsible for creating our own safety and tried strategies, while we are systemically ordered to shut our damn mouths. This is the true magnitude of misogyny's symbiosis with sex work—it is literally criminal for us to openly discuss our work servicing men.

And so I share any information I know about the massage parlor's regular clients with the new girl. Yes, Crybaby appears sober. He can make direct eye contact, and he doesn't have any unidentifiable stains on his clothing. Yes, these are reassuring signs, but otherwise there are no "normal" designations for men who pay for sex. I tell her Crybaby won't negotiate his kinks at the beginning of his session. He'll receive a routine hot oil massage and hand job, and wait until his testicles shrink up before whimpering, "Are you going to hurt me, Mommy? Are you going to hurt me, Mommy?" He doesn't want kind reassurance; nor does he want to be dominated. He needs nothing but to vocalize the words "Are you going to hurt me, Mommy" at the precise moment of ejaculation.

"What a creep," the new girl says.

"He's my favorite client," I tell her.

It's not pity that gains my favor; it's admiration. I'm in awe of his unapologetic honesty and wholeness of sexual expression. If our circumstances were different, and he wasn't a paying client, I would ask him to teach me his secrets. How has his traumatized body made tears and ejaculate into revered equals?

East Vancouver, 2001

My older leatherdyke lover shares her knowledge in a crude language I recognize. "If the demons are always stuck in your head," she knocks her tattooed knuckles on her forehead, "why not willingly invite the demons into the bedroom?" This lover is the teacher I've been searching for. She introduces me to the idea that trauma play, or kinky trauma reenactments, can be used to train the nervous system to respond differently to triggers, to re-teach the brain to make positive new associations with arousal and shame. This makes sense to me; I've always been rough and kinky. Maybe my kinky desires have been offering me a means to heal all along.

We negotiate a scene: I wear a flannel nightie. I drink a faux-dosed mug of warm milk and slip into faux-sedation. My much larger leatherdyke lover's body weight "nearly suffocates" me, and I assume the role of a child-sized victim. She fucks me on a shag carpet while *The Tonight Show Starring Johnny Carson* plays in the background. At the sound of Ed McMahon's long drawn-out "ee" in "Here's Johnny," followed by that optimistic jazz trumpet, I allow myself to experience repulsion and arousal. I cry and gag. I orgasm and grow small with the shame of it. I don't separate out one set of feelings or sensations. The scene ends with my lover smearing hot lube and stage blood between my thighs, leaving me to faux–wake up to the monotone of the NBC broadcast sign-off signal, soiled and alone.

Except, I am not alone. She is on standby in the hallway with a warm blanket and a water bottle, waiting for my cue to reenter the room. As my lover and I debrief, I realize the true power of our trauma play scene—I was everything. A wet mark on the carpet is proof of my orgasm. My tender throat as I sip water from the bottle reminds me I was crying. My lover's steadfast arms around me tell me that I am okay; I am desired and okay and I belong with her. Everything I want to be, and everything I didn't choose to be but am, are present.

This insight crystalizes as I seek out other survivors at play parties and kink conferences. Locating myself within these communities gifts me far more than the validation for wanting the everything feeling I found with my leatherdyke. Kink introduces me to a well-established common credo to lean on: trauma and healing and desire and discomfort are not at odds with each other. Indeed, nothing we are is at odds with another thing that we are, so long as we consciously invite everything together. I witness leather folk celebrating this credo, not just individually but cooperatively. Aha moment. We can be everything, and we can be everything together.

Traveling between Montreal and New York, 2015
I am reading an unabridged English reprint of Violette Leduc's *Thérèse and Isabelle*. I had been waiting for this particular banned book to appear in circulation. I own a retro videotape copy of Radley Metzger's film adaptation of *Thérèse and Isabelle*, a sexploitation production that film critic Roger Ebert pronounced the worst movie of 1968. Whereas many cult followers laud the nonsensical narration and low-production aesthetics that hallmark the sexploitation genre, I look specifically for arousing variations on a theme that I call cunts and catastrophe—or

muffs and malcontent, boobs and burdens, tits and torment (add to this alliterated list of reclaimed words as
you like).

So as I read *Thérèse and Isabelle* in one sitting on an
Amtrak train, it is not to observe a nearly lost text from the
lesbian canon (though it is worthwhile as such); rather, I
am greedy for more cunts and catastrophe, for depictions
of desire and discomfort paired together. Leduc's writing
voraciously displays this theme. Her schoolgirl sweetheart
characters are as antagonistic as they are amorous. Again
and again, they couple physical intimacy with acts of desperate cruelty: "We squeezed each other until we nearly
suffocated. Our hands shaking... our arms fell back, our
inadequacy astonished us... 'Harder, harder, squeeze,' she
demanded." These doomed sex scenes titillate me. I curl
my body toward the passenger window so that the stranger
sitting in the next aisle can't see the blissful expression on
my face. What pleases me most as I read is when Thérèse,
postcoital, talks about her mother. A hostile mother, a
mother with appallingly unhealthy boundaries, a mother
character that closely resembles Leduc's own childhood
abuser, who Leduc wrote unflinchingly about in her well-
known memoir *La Bâtarde*. Like my own writing, Leduc's
memoir and fiction sound strikingly alike.

And like Leduc's Thérèse character, I feel the presence of
my mother when I'm with a lover. In truth, the mere propo-
sition of sex can conjure my mother, or as the case may be,
each and every abuser, including those who failed to protect
me. My associative mind and my traumatized body are so
good at linking arousal and cruelty. Cunts and catastrophe

describes how I view my sexuality to a greater degree than any of the appellations regularly found in my author bio.

I chronically seek movies and books with themes that combine trauma with outlier sexualities. I want to belong, to create space, with those who share my desires, aesthetics, and observations. Sadly, this type of belonging hasn't been as easy to find as small-town sluts who share cigarettes and sex advice. Many of my most cherished titles—the works of art in which I most see myself reflected—have been censored or banned.

Director Louis Malle's *Pretty Baby*, which won the Palme d'Or at Cannes in 1978, debuted a twelve-year-old Brooke Shields in the role of a child prostitute, and was banned in Ontario, where I grew up. John Waters's queer cult classic *Pink Flamingos* was censored across Canada. Actress-turned-director Anjelica Huston's made-for-television adaptation of *Bastard out of Carolina* was banned in Canada, despite its all-star cast and Emmy and Television Critics Association awards. I am particularly devoted to the film *Bastard out of Carolina*, as I am devoted to the original semi-autobiographical novel by self-identified femme lesbian survivor Dorothy Allison. The paperback copy of *Bastard out of Carolina* on my shelf is a treasured possession, passed down to me by a feminist mentor. In turn, I routinely pass along copies to other young women.

In Allison's memoir *Two or Three Things I Know for Sure*, she addresses messages she received for writing concurrently about trauma and sex: "Sex and violence, love and hatred. I'm not ever supposed to put together the two halves of my life—the man who walked across my childhood

and the life I have made for myself... [as a] lesbian, dyke...
and perversely lustful." I've drawn hearts around this passage (yes, fucking hearts).

Violette Leduc's publishing house withheld *Thérèse and
Isabelle* in 1954, and Leduc later disclosed that she contem-
plated suicide while waiting to find out whether her book
would be released or banned. One of Sapphire's earliest
published poems, "Wild Thing," which was printed in a
journal funded by the National Endowment for the Arts,
was circulated in Congress by then-senator Jesse Helms
as an example of "filth and blasphemy." Still, Sapphire
published two poetry collections and a novel that bridged
trauma and sexuality: *American Dreams*, *Black Wings &
Blind Angels*, and *Push*. I routinely pull *Black Wings & Blind
Angels* from my bookshelf, randomly select a page and read
aloud whichever poem is before me. I think about how
these brilliant, trauma-informed, life-affirming poems
could have been silenced, and I read aloud to thank Sapphire for her sexy survivor voice.

I also often think about all the emerging artists, filmmak-
ers, and authors with their own stories of trauma and healing,
stories of brazen sexualities and nonconforming identities,
stories of nuances and complexities that divest from the
dominant narrative entirely. What space have we made—
in the art world and in the larger world—for their stories?

Whistler, 2013
I hate life-changing guided retreats, yet I am naked in a hot
tub with a dozen other women and a certified sex educator,
discussing the ecstatic weekend before us.

I quickly establish myself as the resistant retreat goer. When we go around in a circle sharing our individual goals, I recite a list of no-gos that range from no touching my nipples to no playing any music from the seventies, not even Queen. In many ways, I haven't changed much since I came out. Kinky, sex-positive queers are my people, but I remain more boundaried than most of my friends and lovers.

"Boundaries are beautiful," says the educator.

We all nod in affirmation.

Over the weekend, we write love letters to ourselves and have scheduled cuddle piles beside the fireplace. Miraculously, no one is dairy intolerant and we feed one another fancy cheese and creamy pastries. We blindfold ourselves and participate in a ninety-minute multisensory trance dance, during which I only peeked once—okay, twice. Some of us receive sensual anal massages; others take a fist-fucking and scream right down to the cervix. Whenever I am overwhelmed, I look out at the mountains and breathe. I am actually doing that radical self-care thing. I am happy and present.

So happy and present that I approach an exercise called genital puppet show with uncharacteristic willingness. The exercise involves spreading our legs before the group and telling a story from the perspective of our genitals. *I've got this*, I think. *I practically tell stories for a living.* I hop onto the dining room table—our impromptu puppet stage—and immediately burst into a giggle fit. I pinch my labia majora and make my lips comically open and close like a vertical talking puppet mouth. I laugh. My retreat mates laugh and cheer supportively. I laugh harder, then recognize I'm veering into delirium. I crane my head downward and see the small lumpy scar tissue where my thigh meets my groin and I grow dizzy. Scar tissue I spent hundreds of dollars trying to remove with laser therapy. Continuing to puppet my labia, I say, "The truth is I'm still in so much pain."

For the remainder of the weekend I cycle through trigger responses. I call my wife and make them remind me I'm loved and why they married me. I monopolize the washroom to nurse a sudden flare-up of irritable bowels. I withdraw from the group and retreat into my own catastrophizing thoughts.

"Most of us here are survivors," one of my retreat mates reminds me, consolingly. "We're not afraid of your pain. We're used to it." And it does help to remember I am not alone.

For our closing exercise, the educator asks each of us to plan a personalized fifteen-minute scene that involves both touch and verbal affirmation. I check in with the other women in my group. "I want to pretend I'm some sort of a star athlete, like a football quarterback or boxer maybe?" If anyone is surprised at my scene choice, they hide it well. "It's right after a winning game and all of you will play my coach and teammates." Together, we negotiate a scene of rough shoulder slapping and ass patting, a Gatorade shower, and some wet-towel action. "And I want you to yell things like, 'You did it, champ' and 'We won' and 'We beat them all.'"

I remind myself that most of these strong, sexy women, who've spent the weekend laying bare and loving their bodies, are survivors. "I want to hear us say it, even if it's just a role-play scene," I tell them. "I want to hear us say we won."

East Vancouver, 2017
I understand now that my body holds the story. Kinky and queer sexual expression, including my favorite books and films, have given me all I need to stay connected to the vastness of myself. I reclaimed pleasure and my orgasm through kink. The artists I most admire have modeled ways to hold embodied survivor truths and craft together.

I know I've written something of consequence when my body gets involved: muscle spasms, crying, hunger pains, arousal, and maybe cumming. I will not dissociate from this desire, this physical urge, as I once might have. What I continue to have in common with my younger self, though, is that what specifically makes me feel aroused also still triggers me. I am working through a delicate scene in my novel that describes the sexual abuse of a child character. I write about what the abuser's breath smells like, I describe the texture of his beard against the child character's skin, and my cunt drools through my pajamas and onto my office chair as I tick away at the keyboard.

Briefly, I consider where in my apartment is the best location for a triggered jerk-off. Maybe I shouldn't bring this complex arousal into the bed I share with my wife of ten years? I could run a bath and let my orgasm empty down the drain after I have finished?

I choose the walk-in closet. The dim six-by-four-foot space smells faintly of shoe polish and lavender fabric softener. I kneel with my knees splayed as far apart as the shoe-cluttered floor will allow, rest my head in an open drawer of neatly folded underwear. I want this jerk-off to achieve the same temporal particularity, the same quality of idiosyncratic detail that I use when I negotiate a scene with a play partner or write a scene in my novel.

My body always deserves a good story. Now, the story goes something like this: I submit to the enormity of my life. I belong in circles of small-town sluts and kinky queers. And with survivors, who remind each other we're never alone. And I belong to myself. I will read as part of my healing. I will always write, and I believe my books will find their way to readers who need them. I will thank my traumatized body for being my wisest teacher. I will touch and affirm myself, especially when it's painful. My body holds the story. My body is the story.

A SISTER BY WATER, A SISTER BY BLOOD

·

Soraya Palmer

•

ELEVEN YEARS AGO I turned twenty-two. By this time, two of my three sisters were dead. The first was killed by an ex-boyfriend. She was found strangled and face smashed. Her body had been left for three days in an empty apartment. Her corpse was found only because the neighbors could smell her body rotting in the New York City heat. The second was killed by grief, trauma, isolation, and alcohol. To be clear, it was not the second sister's body that died, just the person that I knew—the one who had once been my whole world.

I WANT TO be able to tell you a story about these deaths, yet it also seems reductive—to attempt to fabricate meaning and symbolism out of something as complex and contradictory as a life. When the first sister, Amahle,* died, we all tried to make meaning out of it. Her death became the way we fell apart. We told stories about her to comfort

---

* All names have been changed.

ourselves—stories to make meaning out of her death, her life. I don't want to reduce Amahle's life, her death, my grief into stories. But I also must admit that I'm a story-teller. I don't know how to tell without telling stories. So instead of telling one story about Amahle's death, I will tell you several.

"WE THINK WE tell stories, but stories often tell us," Rebecca Solnit once wrote. My sister Karina and I were once great storytellers. When we were young, we were our only world. We were all that mattered. We called our world Ivclonia, which meant Land of the Fairies. We planned to make it into an animated film eventually. We tried to write our world down into a book. Half I wrote; half she wrote. I don't remember who wrote what. She wound up taking over and creating newer darker worlds without me.

In our first rendition, the fairies save the children, and then the children save the fairies back. In our world, the children and the fairies both got to be heroes, and they both got to be saved.

But at some point, the ending changed. The fairies were all killed. The children, in their innocent quest to find Iv-clonia and help the fairies, unknowingly created a trail that other humans later followed. Of course, the humans only wanted the magic for themselves. The one remaining fairy was fed to a human, who became a new, very evil species that set off a new, very dark period.

Years later, after our worlds and our sisterhood had fallen apart, I looked everywhere for these worlds, but I couldn't find them anywhere. Looking back at our revised ending, I wonder if there was something our imaginations knew that the rest of us didn't. A darkness on the horizon.

We don't create a fantasy world to escape reality.
We create it to be able to stay.

—LYNDA BARRY

IN 2001, KARINA came home from the first day of her summer school program and announced that she had just met a girl named Amahle who thought that everything was hilarious. I was sixteen. Karina and Amahle were both freshmen. According to Karina, they had just decided to become friends on that day, which was Amahle's birthday— or the anniversary, as they would soon refer to it. When Karina met Amahle, I was jealous. I am ashamed to admit this, but it's true. Karina had found a new best friend, and it wasn't me.

THE FIRST TIME I really hung out with Amahle, the three of us were in my parents' room watching television when this Walmart commercial came on with a yellow smiley face that suddenly started singing. The singing smile became so big that it eventually covered the entire face and almost the entire screen. Karina and I thought it was pretty trite, but Amahle just sat there cracking up—just like Karina said she would—and she wouldn't stop. Even though the jokes were never actually funny, I was always a little jealous that I couldn't see the humor in everyday events the way that she could.

AMAHLE WAS THE only person besides Karina who knew about my imaginary boyfriend. People would see us in the halls and ask if we three were sisters, and so we were. Just like that, Amahle entered our world.

WHEN I WENT to my senior prom, Amahle and Karina were jealous that I had a prom to go to and they didn't. I didn't tell them that I didn't want to go—that I didn't have any friendships quite like theirs at school, or anywhere else for that matter. It would've been too uncool. They made their own "prom" video where they dressed up in my clothes and danced around the house and showed it to me the next day. I still believe that their night was more fun than mine, and they agreed.

ONE STORY IS this: Amahle died eleven years ago. And when she did, I lost my best friend.

I should clarify that Amahle was not my best friend. She was Karina's, and Karina was mine. And when Karina lost Amahle, I lost them both. One I lost literally, and one I lost in another way.

Sometimes when a person dies, they start to live inside you, and you look to them and away from the people in your life.

Sometimes when a person gets taken over by grief, their face transforms, their eyes become glass; you wave your hand over their eyes to see if their face still registers your presence.

THE FIRST STORY of Amahle's death is the simplest one. It is where I was when she died.

Of course I couldn't have known that the day I chose to leave my home in New York City to volunteer for a year in Honduras would wind up being just one day before my sister by water and not by blood would be killed by a man who once slept in my house, whom I cooked eggs for. It is a day that I replay in my head again and again. Amahle, the water sister, and I were on the phone. She wanted Karina, my sister by blood, and me to attend a party. I was packing my bags to leave the country. Karina stayed to help. I would be gone for a year. It would be the longest I'd ever spent away from home.

"A year goes by so fast. We'll see each other in no time," Amahle said. I tried to hide my longing to see her by performing cheeriness—a defense mechanism of mine. Her voice had a familiar loud optimism that often made me wonder if we shared the same defense mechanism. This was the last time I would ever speak to Amahle.

I had recently graduated from college and I was too young and naïve to understand the arrogant blindness of leaving your country to go volunteer, to "help" people in another country with a different culture and language. Looking back on this year, I can see more clearly now that even my desire to help others was more about me than them. I wanted to be important. I wanted to be remembered. I wanted to be good at something. I thought maybe I was good at helping. In August 2007, I signed a yearlong contract. My family gave me their blessing.

The day I got the news was the day the girl known to

staff simply as *malcriado* threw stones at my face for being a *sope*—the word they used for vulture—because we shared the same color skin. I was the only Black volunteer on the ranch. The few Black children there were quick to denounce their African ancestry because of years of colonial conditioning. It was my fifth day living at the orphanage. The phone connection was so bad I could only hear every other word. "What?" I kept asking. The only word I could make out for sure was "dead." Finally, I heard the other word: "Amahle."

THIS IS THE story the world made of her death. My family didn't tell me how Amahle died because they didn't want to worry me. I spent the next twelve hours on the internet searching for clues. There were pictures of her in every newspaper: the *New York Times, New York Daily News, Village Voice.* Often she was pictured with him—the man who killed her—looking young and in love. She was shown with cheap drinks in her hand, the dark makeup she started wearing more often, and a spark of teenage recklessness in her eyes. Newspapers by nature are meant to create a narrative—a progression of order and logic—out of facts that may not make true sense. Here is some of what they said:

> An unemployed and sometimes homeless security guard charged with strangling the daughter of New York University professors told investigators that he had been jealous because she invited other men but not him to her party, prosecutors said in court papers released yesterday.
> —*New York Times*

> Amahle (20) was murdered and found rotting in her
> Greenwich Village apartment surrounded by condom
> wrappers.—*New York Post*

A GUY I remembered only as a pothead I went to high
school with was in film school and wanted to know if he
could interview me for the documentary he was making; it
can now be found on IMDb.com. The tagline reads: "A documentary about a young woman murdered by her former
boyfriend in New York in 2007 told through home movies,
stills, and interviews with her family and friends."

> A chilling account of pure innocence marred by pure evil!
> —anonymous IMDb commenter

I WAS ON the plane back to New York for the memorial.
I couldn't afford to go to the funeral in South Africa. The
woman sitting next to me told me about how she'd just read
the most horrible news story in the *New York Times* about a
beautiful woman killed in her NYU apartment by her crazy
ex-boyfriend.

IMAGINE A WHOLE life suddenly summed up in rumors
and adjectives: "party girl," "binge drinker," "daddy issues."
The girl pictured and written about in the news articles
resembled my friend—but was different. They made her
look shallow, hollow, asking for trouble.

This is the story they always tell about women who are
raped and killed by the men in their lives. I want to blame
the media, but I wonder why it is that we keep wanting to

be told this story. The story tells us that there must always be a reason they died. There must be something to separate the women who die from the women who don't—because the idea that it can truly happen to any of us, that our world does not make sense, is too troubling for most of us to accept entirely.

> Even the man's defense lawyer wept. So did the man as he turned to apologize to the family. "I know what I did was wrong," he said. Yet he failed to offer an explanation for the brutal crime. "It was just something that happened," he shrugged, after declaring his undying love for the victim.
> —*New York Daily News*

I LOGGED ON to Facebook later that day and, just hours after hearing the news, received the following message: "Hi, my name is Meredith Leitch. I work for *North Star* magazine. I'm messaging all of Amahle's Facebook friends wondering if you could give me some information on your take of the murder. When did you sense that the man who killed Amahle was capable of such vile atrocities?"

WHEN I CLOSE my eyes, I replay my last conversation with Amahle. I change the ending. Karina and I finish packing early and make it to Amahle's party after all. We spend the night at her place, as we often did. When the man who killed her arrives the next morning, Karina and I are there to protect her. The man feels nervous having so many witnesses and decides not to go through with it—or he tries to attack and we call security downstairs and they rush in with guns—or we find her right after he leaves and there's still time and we rush her to the hospital. The doctor tells us she's in stable condition; it was a miracle.

WHEN YOU'RE FAR away when someone dies, it's like they're not really dead. I never saw the body. Where I was, nobody knew Amahle. I fell asleep hearing her voice at night. When I closed my eyes, I swore I could feel her everywhere. I woke up every morning thinking maybe, just maybe, there was still time to save her.

There are times even now when I still don't believe that she's really dead.

ONE TIME AT a party, I got drunk and decided to slap the man who would eventually kill her in the face. I didn't know what had come over me. I had a feeling about him, a terrible feeling that I never shared with anyone whenever I saw the man. I'd be lying if I said I knew he would kill her. But I would also be lying if I said that I ever thought she was safe with him.

We'd only heard about one prior incident. About a month before Amahle died, the man who killed her stole her passport and dragged her across the ground by her hair outside of her dorm room. There were many witnesses. This was the first time we had proof that the man was physically abusive.

When she went to the police to get her passport back they told her there was nothing they could do. They looked at the bruises across her arms and legs and told her they needed more facts before investigating the situation. She decided to leave him. We were relieved. We thought the worst was behind us.

A study on intimate partner violence (IPV) states that one in ten IPV-related homicide victims "experienced some form of violence in the month before their death, suggesting an opportunity for intervention." It is a fact that makes you go back and retrace all of the possible interventions you could have made.

I try to convince myself over and over again that even if I didn't get on that plane to Honduras, even if we did go to her party that night, even if we were there when the man came to the door, that we might not have been able to stop him, that he might've killed us too.

But most of the time I think it's me who killed her.

I TOO WANT to make sense of her death. If there was truly nothing I could have done, why do I still want to save her? Maybe selflessness is like martyrdom, like a masochist in disguise. The advice dating violence prevention organizations always give is never tell a battered woman to leave her batterer. But once she's dead that's all you'll ever wish you did.

One of the last memories I have of Amahle was when I went to stay with her and Karina in Karina's college apartment. Amahle had recently split open her leg, attempting to climb through the window to the roof. Her entire leg had turned purple. I thought she might need stitches. It was unsettling—watching the wide-openness of her smile contrasted with her purple leg. She was so happy that she'd finally broken things off with the man who would kill her.

She changed her phone number, her Myspace and Facebook passwords. She was a free woman. "Everything will be different now," she said. "You'll see."

OF COURSE, THE reason that they tell you not to tell a survivor to leave their abuser—besides the fact that it won't work—is that the moment the victim leaves her abuser is actually the most likely time for her to be killed by them. This is the reason for things like safety planning, domestic violence shelters, name changes. Had we known this, maybe we could have tried harder to convince her not to be in that apartment by herself all summer. Maybe we could have taken her somewhere that he could never find her. All we could tell in that moment was that she should leave. And I can't help but think that if we had spent more time listening, less time anxiously wanting her to leave him, that maybe we could have saved her.

THIS IS WHERE I was when Karina died. We were sitting in her bedroom. Sketches of the new fairy world she had created called Mitra were on the ground, on the walls, growing upwards. They were all you could see. Like a scene from *Where the Wild Things Are*, her room had become a blueprint for her mind—both an escape and a means to stay in the world where her best friend was dead.

In this period, I rarely saw her leave her room, but there were remnants left of her throughout our house. Like a ghost, she haunted me. I couldn't stop thinking she might be next. I had dreams of waking up to headlines like the ones I found about Amahle, summing up her life with empty descriptors:

Here lies Karina, age 23, found rotting, in her childhood bedroom, watching Korean soap operas.

I don't know how to explain it, but every tragedy, every death, somehow reminded me of her. The comparisons had become absurd.

I watched *Hotel Rwanda* and the mass grave of children took on Karina's face.

How do you tell someone you feel you lost them when someone else is truly dead in a coffin somewhere without sounding selfish and insane?

The day our sisterhood died I sat down next to her, looked for some trace of her inside her face, but I did not see Karina there. It was like when I was young and she was just born, and I would sometimes worry that her body had been taken over by an alien. I'd look at her face until I was convinced it was her. If I wasn't convinced, I would cry until our parents came.

This time, years later, I looked at her. I said her name, "Karina," and she looked back at me, expressionless. She looked like she'd been abducted again. This time by grief.

I thought about Amahle. How many times had I wanted to tell her to leave him? I never told Amahle to leave the man who killed her. I never told her parents. I never told mine. I never told her how much the man scared me. I never even told her that I would miss her when I was in Honduras.

It's only now that I realize my fear over losing Karina was really a mask for my guilt over losing Amahle. I thought if I could save Karina, I would be saving Amahle too.

I decided to show our parents the bottles under Karina's bed. They asked me why I hadn't told them sooner. They told me now it was too late; Karina was already gone. My mother threw away Karina's drawings. They poured out the bottles from under her bed.

Shortly after, Karina and I collided. She felt betrayed I told our parents. But I felt betrayed too.

WHEN AMAHLE DIED, Karina told me that she had to stop dancing because it reminded her too much of Amahle. We didn't dance together again for some time. I wanted to say, "But wasn't it you who taught me to dance? Who insisted we record our performances to show to our family before we even knew Amahle existed?" I felt betrayed by this because I had danced with Karina first. This is clear to me now. I didn't want Karina to love a person more than she loved me, and I wondered if this made me no different from the man who killed Amahle after learning that she did not wish to belong to him.

Love is never any better than the lover. Wicked people love wickedly, violent people love violently, weak people love weakly, stupid people love stupidly, but the love of a free man is never safe. There is no gift for the beloved.

—TONI MORRISON

THE MAN WHO killed Amahle wrote her poetry every day. Amahle called him passionate. The newspapers called her death a crime of passion.

The word "passion" comes from the Latin verb "to suffer" or "to endure." Passion is an "intense, driving, or overmastering feeling or conviction; an outbreak of anger, something that differentiates from reason." In the Bible, "the Passion" refers to the suffering that Christ endured between the Last Supper and his death.

I want to know a more radical form of loving than this. But it is difficult to love in any way that is different from the way you yourself have been loved.

THE MAN WHO killed Amahle had lost both his parents, had been failed by the state, had lived on the streets, had been in and out of jail, had been labeled a criminal by so many in his life, including me.

The *New York Post* referred to the man as a beast and to Amahle as "the beauty." And although I can see through the classism and racism that dehumanized the man in these articles, and presumably throughout his life, it is hard for me to see him the way Amahle saw him—as completely and fully human. It is hard for me to want to. Even now, I cannot bear to tell you his name. I don't wish to see it written here. I don't wish to hear it repeated back to me in conversations.

I can see clearly how loving someone in a certain way can be passionate, can be violent, can be a hatred storming inside you. Had I seen the man who killed her the day I got the news, I would have tried to kill him myself. And I think that the very idea that people who do bad things should go to prison to be punished—to serve justice—comes from the pleasure we get in seeing those who have wronged us suffer.

Yet, still, I remember seeing a photo of the man in court with his sister, whom he had been staying with when he was homeless. I heard that his sister was pregnant at the time. Her face looked broken. I wondered what it must have been like to be this woman: to lose her parents, to grow up without financial stability, to be seen by society as the daughter of a "welfare queen"—only to lose her brother to a distorted, heartbroken rage. A rage that probably could have been avoided had he not lived in a world that criminalized him from the day he was born. I saw the heartbreak in her face. I thought, *What would her face have looked like if I had killed him?*

The day I collided with Karina, I was heartbroken that I was losing her. Yet in the process of trying to save her, I nearly killed her too. Our fight ended with me throwing a glass vase at her face, which broke and cut an artery in her arm and landed her in the emergency room. The doctor told her that if the glass had gone in any deeper, she would have died on her way to the hospital.

When my brother came home, he said our kitchen looked like a murder scene. Glass and blood were everywhere.

The truth is that I don't remember throwing the vase at all. My mind has blanked it out entirely.

All I remember is the pain I felt that I had been keeping inside me all that time and that exploded on my sister that day in our kitchen. If I had killed her, I would be the monster too. Not sitting here writing this essay, working with high school students on conflict de-escalation.

AFTER THE FIGHT, my parents said to me, "This isn't like you. We need you to be the strong one here. We need you to be the glue."

I found a journal entry that I wrote to record my feelings that day:

I am still afraid of falling asleep at night and watching her drown. Even as glue I cannot hold her. You cannot save someone who wants to stay in the water.

"It's fine," she says. "I like the waves as they wash over me. That numb feeling the water gives me, the redness in my eyes from the salty salt. I like it down here. No, I don't want to come up for air."

And so I let her drown.

Even as glue I could not save her.

THE THING THEY don't tell you about death is that everyone blames themselves and each other, and suddenly you're not a family anymore.

The thing about Black families is they go on forever. Every friend becomes an auntie. Amahle became a sister, and sister a soul mate.

When Amahle died, we blamed ourselves, each other, and even Amahle herself for dying. Karina kept Amahle's ashes in an urn that she wore around her neck for years.

All I keep are memories. Something I cannot hold.

I can only find one photo of me and Amahle. It was the time we did a modeling shoot for a friend where we lay on a bathroom floor pouring water over our faces. It is not a great photo, but it is the one tangible piece of our friendship that I have. I keep it on my desktop.

Rebecca Solnit wrote that sometimes our stories tell us, and I think the story I needed to be told was that Amahle's death was never my fault, that she knew how much I loved her, that she was okay now, somewhere he could never hurt her.

BUT WHAT ARE the stories Amahle told about herself?

On her Myspace page Amahle wrote that her first name "means happiness, which I guess fits my personality, 'cause I laugh really loud and obnoxiously—all the time. I'm a South African baby."

This was on Amahle's Facebook profile the day she died: "Over the last year I have developed a ZERO-tolerance for bullshit, so please take that shit elsewhere! (No exceptions). I love my friends and family who are ALWAYS there for me! They mean everything to me!! I'm a friendly person, but don't be fooled into mistaking it for weakness!"

Below was this quote from Audre Lorde: "For to survive in the mouth of this dragon we call America, we have had to learn this first and most vital lesson—that we were never meant to survive."

AMAHLE DID NOT want to die. She was passionate about prisoners' rights and dreamed of becoming president. She wanted to travel and to love and to be loved deeply. I don't think she ever thought the man who killed her would do it. But maybe she knew that he could. Or that like the time she went to the police when he stole her passport, the systems were stacked against her, that there was little she could do.

Still, it's alarming the number of people I've met who blame Amahle for her death.

In reality, of course, the leading cause of death for American women is that their boyfriends and husbands kill them. And Black women make up the highest percentage of casualties.

But as Black women, we also know how to hold each other to the light. When I told Karina I was writing this essay, she told me not to show it to her because she didn't want to read it. But she also told me that she needed me to write this essay.

A funny thing that happens when you stop trying to save people is that they start to save themselves. A few years ago, Karina moved out of New York, began a new healthy relationship, went back to school, managed a 4.0 GPA, started exercising, bought a dog, and began regularly doing monthly health cleanses.

I wasn't sure that I wanted to tell you a story, that I wanted to make Amahle's life and death mean something to you as a reader, that I wanted you to be entertained by these words. Yet here we are with a happy ending.

Karina was never dead. She was mourning, which I saw as a death. I was mourning, but without allowing myself to acknowledge my grief, I became my own killer. Karina's killer too.

Our fight forced us to confront each other and our own heartbreak in ways we hadn't done before. Karina and I were forced to create new worlds. At first I thought I lost her to hers. And then a bridge was created and we walked over to meet one another there.

Karina is the first person I think of when I feel that I am nothing. And every summer—during the season when Amahle died—Karina and I celebrate Sisters Day. A day we created when we celebrate our lives, our friendship. When we try to reenter a world where fairies can be saved by children and violence and death can be prevented by believing in magic, in love, and in sisters.

NOT OVER IT, NOT FIXED, AND LIVING A LIFE WORTH LIVING:

A DISABILITY JUSTICE VISION OF SURVIVORHOOD

•

Leah Lakshmi
Piepzna-Samarasinha

•

To all survivors today: your time is precious,
your energy is precious, you are precious. Your love is
precious, your relationships are precious. And I
don't mean precious like cute. I mean precious like invaluable,
like massive, like power, like transcendent.

—HANNAH HARRIS-SUTRO

Healing is dangerous work. Healing is about going into the
struggle. When trauma happens, we go away from that
space in our body where it happened—and when we go into it,
it hurts so much as it wakes back up. I'm interested in
creating the place where the body can remember itself, even
though it hurts to do it. Where feeling better is part of it,
but it's not the goal. Struggling better is the goal.

—SUSAN RAFFO

unfixed, evading capture

Recently, I was auditioning a new therapist, who asked me in all sincerity during the intake if I thought the therapy I'd gotten in my twenties had "resolved my childhood sexual abuse."

I had high hopes for this therapist. She was a woman of color with a Cesar Chavez quote on her website. She worked at the local healing justice center staffed entirely by people of color healers. She said she was "trauma-informed" on her website and listed working with survivors as one of her areas of expertise. Plus, she was cheaper than the therapist I'd been seeing for seven years, who was one of the smartest, weirdest healers I'd ever met, but still lived in Oakland, where I'd been priced out. Maybe seeing a therapist in person, not via Skype, would be a good thing?

But there I was, in the office with my mouth slightly open and the rug pulled out from under me. As it turned out, we had some really different understandings of trauma, healing, and survivorhood. She really thought that childhood sexual abuse was something to manage, something you could get over and "move on" from, a cut that could be stitched up with butterfly bandages. Not: *My abuse isn't something to resolve, a number on a pain scale, a simple wound that can go away with Neosporin. My trauma is an opera, a gorgeous and tough dress made out of my best scars, a seed library, a Gutenberg Bible, a thunderstorm to climb and buck in a small plane, a mountain range, a supernova to map.*

It's trauma. It's also a resource. A resource that isn't just an individual one, but one that connects me to other survivors and their collective knowledge. Knowledge that we have used to survive, and that we could potentially use to change the world, end rape culture, and create new forms of healing, family, communication, and justice.

When I composed myself, I managed to say, "I don't really think of it like that. I think that I'm on a lifelong journey of learning from and healing my trauma. You know what I mean?" *You know what I mean, right?*

She smirked at me with that poor-dear-sure-let-her-think-that look. And I didn't go back.

THE IDEA THAT survivorhood is a thing to fix, cure, or get over, and that a cure is not only possible and easy but is the only desirable option, is a foundational belief in mainstream ways of understanding survivorhood and survivors. And the idea of survivorhood as solely an unfortunate condition to cure is an idea with deep roots in ableism.

Ableism believes that when there's something "wrong" with a body/mind, the only desirable outcome to that wrongness is cure. It also believes that you can either be fixed or broken—there's nothing in between. It certainly believes that there is nothing valuable in inhabiting a body/mind that's disabled.

The idea of "getting over it" is also deeply seductive to survivors. We want the pain and trauma of surviving sexual abuse or assault to be over. Who wouldn't? What's the problem with that?

AS I WRITE this essay, the #MeToo movement has toppled senators, movie moguls, and many other famous white men (and some Black and brown ones), but more importantly, it's created an explosion of survivors telling our stories. A movement created in 2007 by Black survivor activist Tarana Burke, #MeToo encouraged survivors to break silence about the rape and abuse we'd survived and was then Columbus-ed by several white North American cis lady media figures in late 2017. But #MeToo also took on a life of its own, claimed by many everyday survivors as a strategy to make space for us to speak, argue, and organize around survivorhood in all its complex iterations.

The thing I like most about #MeToo is how it, for a moment at least, transformed the experience of being a survivor from one that—despite me being embedded in survivor culture—still so often feels freakish and lonely, to one where the truth is out there: rape and childhood sexual abuse are the norm and *most people* are survivors. #MeToo created space where the weaponization of sex wasn't seen as a rarity or an accidental tragedy befalling a sad handful of people, but as a system of oppression that's everywhere, in the water and the air just like any industrial pollutant.

This is dangerous information. As survivors, we often feel powerless because rape and abuse are an attempt to destroy our power, and we often lack systemic power (when the legal system is racist, whorephobic, inaccessible, and not our vision of justice anyway, when people don't believe our experiences, when we can't afford therapy). But we survivors are also supremely powerful. Our stories of rape and survivorhood are a thundercloud, a nebula. They are huge and awesome and, if spoken, can and do bring rape culture to its knees.

Rape culture and its proponents know this, and it scares the shit out of them. The power our stories have scares the shit out of them. So rape culture creates many things to manage survivor knowledge and tamp it down. Sometimes, I call it the Survivor Industrial Complex: the web of institutions, practices, and beliefs that works to manage, contain, and offer resolution to survivors of sexual violence. Similar to how the nonprofit industrial complex[1] contains and manages dissent. Its reach is huge, stretching from the nurses who administer rape kits, to YWCA therapists who run twelve-week group therapy sessions. From the six-week "solution-focused" therapy that is the only kind available at the sliding scale clinic, to the cops and district attorneys who decide who counts as a "perfect victim," and who is too slutty, poor, Black, brown, crazy, or trans to deserve victim compensation funds.

One of the biggest ways the Survivor Industrial Complex manages all those messy, powerful survivor emotions and truths is by deploying the idea of the good or fixed survivor. The Good Survivor is the survivor you see on a talk show or a soap opera, the one who received three months of therapy and is all better now. The abuse is a vague memory; there are no visible scars—physical or emotional—and they don't talk about the invisible ones. They've moved on. They don't talk about abuse in an ongoing way, ask for accommodations, get triggered during sex, have a new memory, or figure out something else about their trauma years later. They don't ask that survivorhood or trauma be talked about or held in our movements, communities, or queer scenes, or insist that understanding those things could strengthen those movements. They don't bother you with "their drama" or "their stuff," and they know that talking about it for sure would be a bother.

The Good Survivor is someone I've never met in person, because they don't exist. But their archetype haunts me and many other survivors I know. We beat ourselves up for not being them. And often, unfortunately, our partners, friends, co-workers, and comrades want us to be that good, quiet, all-better survivor too.

In contrast, the bad survivor is the one who's still "broken," still freaking out, still triggered, still grieving, still remembering. Still making you remember. They have a panic attack during the action, they think they can perform a certain sexual act but disassociate or throw up anyway, they tell you terrible stories that haunt your dreams, they're pissed off at the local rape crisis center for being racist or transmisogynist or just fucking inadequate. They haven't forgotten shit. Bad survivors see the secret insides of rape culture every day, and talk about it. They're the femme with baggage you scroll past on Tinder because they look like too much drama. They're the survivor who kills themself and who is described later in sorrowful tones as "broken, but now at peace." They're the bitch, the hysteric, the dyke. And often, as survivors, we don't want to be them, because being them means being not healed. It means that we've failed at surviving.

These archetypes are binaries. The world reinforces these stereotypes in a million ways, but we also repeat them to ourselves. We torture ourselves with them, and also—let's be real—they're seductive. They make things feel simple. If we believe that some survivors are just too annoying or bitchy, too out of control, we can feel better about ourselves by promising we're not like *that* and then distancing ourselves from those high-maintenance bitches. And if the promise of ease is a possibility, maybe someday we can achieve it.

THE PROMISE OF a cure for survivorhood is what lies inside the Good Survivor, and it's tempting: most people experiencing pain want it to stop. As a young survivor, I was in torment every single second of every day, and I wanted to get some goddamned peace. I wanted to fuck. I wanted to stop being so gone from my body that the whole world looked like a TV screen. I wanted to not feel like broken glass. I wanted to be able to think or talk about something other than my incest memories twenty-four/seven. I wanted those things because it hurt, and because of the rolled eyes, imagined and real, of the people around me who were impatient about me discussing all that depressing stuff all the time.

And there was more. I wanted to interrupt the cycles of abuse and intergenerational violence in my family. I wanted to grow up to have relationships that weren't violent. To know pleasure, not martyrdom. Most of all, I wanted to be happy, and I wanted to know freedom, joy, and liberation. Even though and especially because I had no idea what those things actually felt like.

These are powerful, fierce survivor freedom dreams. Dreams like these are where I see many survivors in our fiercest power as revolutionaries. There is revolution in survivors remembering the omnipresence of rape, insisting that we remember shit right, and using our deepest dreams to create new worlds that we have never seen.

There's nothing wrong with wanting less pain, or a different experience of it. There's nothing wrong with wanting to transform generations of passed-down trauma. But what gets more complicated is when those desires bleed into the ableist model of cure.[2] That model and its harsh binary of fixed and successful versus broken and fucked is part of what contributes to suicide and struggle in long-term survivors. I've seen survivors, including myself, struggle with feelings of failure and self-hatred when we're thirty, forty, fifty, sixty, or older and we're still triggered, grieving, and remembering, when we haven't reached that mythic cured place. What keeps me alive and thriving is my work as a disabled survivor. Undoing and picking apart that binary and naming its poison as ableist. Bringing together crip and survivor struggles and knowledge. Mapping a new model of survival that charts where my scars and my still being crazy in adulthood are not signs that I've failed.

Cure, Crips, and Survivors
My friend Blyth Barnow is a white, working-class femme survivor priest. A couple of months ago, an Instagram photograph she posted blew me away. It was an image of big flip chart paper in a workshop, with writing that said, "How do survivors' skills translate to ministry?" Underneath, there was a list of words like *boundaries, finding healing moment in texts, nuance, destigmatizing mental health, process of finding healthy self-worth,* and *self-grace.*

Skills. Survivors' skills. Survivors as people who are good at things. Survivors as leaders, because of and not despite our survivorhood. Blyth's post was the first time in my life, after more than twenty years of being deeply integrated in survivor communities, that I'd seen survivors described as being good at things. As having specific skills that emerged from our survivorhood.

There is a deep parallel between the way being a survivor is seen only as a fault, never as a skill, and the way ableism views disabled people as individual, tragic health defects (if you doubt me, think about how disabled fetuses are never referred to as disabled fetuses, but as *birth defects*). When I lead disability justice workshops, one of my toughest teaching moments is always to get people to step out of the deficiency model of disability. When I talk about disabled wisdom and skills, or about disabled people as having histories, cultures, and movements, the blank looks in the room kill me. It's damn near impossible for many abled people to think of disability as anything other than an individual tragedy and a state no one would choose to inhabit.

But I, along with many other disabled people and people who believe in disability justice, insist that disabled people have competencies and skills that abled people lack, like deep knowledge of how to create collective access,[3] compassion, flexibility, ingenuity, and community in which crips, kids, elders, poor people, and families are not just (begrudgingly) included but hold power and set the agenda, leading the march as slowly as we need to. When wildfires spread across most of western North America in the summer and fall of 2017, sick and disabled people already knew how to protect ourselves from smoke. We shared with able-bodied people who were facing air stress for the first time our knowledge of N95 and P95 masks and respirators, air purifiers, and herbs to detox, soothe lungs, and ease anxiety, as well as our crip sense of time where we can only do what we can do.

We've already survived the end of the world, and our knowledge will be what helps us survive any coming apocalypse of fascism and climate change.

But in the deficiency model of disability, there's nothing good about disability—no skills or brilliance—we are just a fault to be cured. The only good crip is a cured crip, one who has ceased to exist. That lack of existence happens through cure. Cure is healing is elimination.

And cure infects survivor dialogues. Survivors longing for healing hit the medical-industrial complex in search of therapy, only to confront the idea of cure as the only way to heal from abuse. This belief breeds shame and promotes the binary of fixed or broken. This binary stops us from being able to imagine survivor futures where we are thriving but not cured.

WHEN I WAS a young survivor, I would ask my counselors when "it" would get better, when "it" would be gone. By "it" I meant something between "having flashbacks every day and feeling constantly in trauma hell" and "having any trauma memories or experiences at all." Something like survivorhood. I was horrified when one gifted and lovely therapist gently told me that "it" would never fully go away, but my life would and could transform so much I wouldn't even recognize it, and my experience of pain, trauma, and abuse memories would also transform.

My counselor was trying, as best she could, to convey what I would later learn through years of listening to and shape-shifting chronic pain: our experiences of pain and trauma can completely transform when we have access to community, tools, support, and different stories and narratives.

But as a young survivor, the vision I was given from most sources—including some therapists and feminist abuse books—was this: if I performed healing correctly, by the time I was thirty or forty, I would be a survivor who had no visible signs of survivorhood. One who wasn't crazy anymore, who never panicked, never jumped when she was touched the wrong way, never flashed back to beliefs she'd been taught about how truly stupid it was to trust anybody, who was never brought to her knees by anger or grief or sadness or fear or freezing. The abuse would be gone, and I would be good as new—or as good as someone who had never been abused. It was a vision of survivorhood that mimicked the Good Survivor archetype, albeit often with a feminist, anti-oppressive coating.

In this worldview, if I ever had flashbacks, trauma, pain, or triggers, that meant I was failing. At survivorhood. At healing. At fixing it. At breaking the cycle. This was my life's work, the thing that everything hung on. This was a terribly hard place to be. And, then and today, I see survivors struggling with feelings of deep shame that we are not "over it." I see survivors in our thirties, forties, and beyond getting thrown into suicidal thoughts when we are triggered, again, because we're beating ourselves up over still being "unfixed." When a new memory or a new experience of trauma or grief comes to us. When we are still sad, still panicking, still crazy. We think we are failing.

I believe that bringing a disability justice[4] analysis of ableism into survivor culture—where struggle and scar are not failures, where our vision of healing shifts from *getting over it* to *still fucked up and also beautiful and okay*—could do a lot to address this struggle. This might be a big leap for many survivors and supporters of survivors. We don't often think of survivorhood within a disability framework, and many people still think of disability in a limited way, as only meaning a small number of people with certain strictly defined physical disabilities. But I define disability as a broader term. "Disabled" is a word/world that includes people with physical disabilities, people who are deaf, hard of hearing, deaf/blind or blind, people who identify as mad/ mentally ill, people who are neuro-divergent, and people with chronic illness. Disability can also be defined as anyone whose body/mind do not conform to oppressive society's notions of "normal" or "functional."

There are many disabled, deaf, blind, chronically ill, and/or neuro-divergent survivors, and I also believe that all survivors of sexual or physical abuse who hold trauma memories and responses, have complex post-traumatic stress disorder, multiplicity/dissociative identity disorder, or other trauma-rooted psychic differences, could find a home in disability communities. The same skills we have developed as crips—asking for collectively created access as a right, not a favor, and resisting ableist ideas of our body/minds

as fucked-up failures—can be a vital part of where we create our reparations and our salvation as survivors.

When we are not fixed, not over it, still triggered, still
feeling, still healing in our forties, fifties, sixties, and
beyond, we are not failing. We are remembering. We are
learning from our survivorhood. We are moving from a
model that gasps at our scars to one that wants to learn
as much from them as possible. We are not an individual
defect. We are a collective movement, a series of overlap-
ping survivor communities.

And I ask the dangerous question: What if more survivors—and the therapists and healing spaces available
to us—had a mad, crip idea of healing, one that was not
about cure but about increasing possibility, about learning,
about loving all our survivor mad genius? What if there
were models and stories where we got to grieve as long
as we needed to? Where we had tools to hold the grief?
Where that grief was seen as sacred and valuable, a source
of life-giving knowledge, not a pain in the ass? What if bad
survivors were good survivors? What if all survivors were
beautiful in our mess?

Old-Ass Survivors Who Cry and Laugh

As a young survivor, I read a lot of survivor writing—the
feminist of color slam poetry kind, the Dorothy Allison
kind. What I picked up on was that telling the raw truth
could heal you. Running away could heal you. Cutting off
someone's dick could heal you (thank God Lòrena Bobbitt
was in the news when I was twenty). Sex could heal you,
and solitude, and a closed door, and collective houses, and
herbs. Time and space and silence.

What I didn't see much of was stories of what came after, what long-term survivorhood looked like after you'd been trying to heal for a while.

It would've meant a lot to me, I think, if I'd seen stories and pictures of some middle-aged or even older survivor femmes who were happy and yet, not done. Who were a lot less triggered than they used to be, but still snapped at their partner, froze up when touched a certain way, had a great month and then a week of panic attacks and then just had to get the fuck out of town for a while. Who were successful on their own terms and who also had at least a few deeply shitty mental health times a year. Who had chosen queer family that was wonderful, the best, and also fell the fuck apart in completely unpredictable and disastrous ways. Who thought they knew everything about their abuse story, but who then woke up one day at forty-two and thought, *Shit, maybe my mom also abused my older cousin who was like me and who she also had a "special closeness" to*, or realized, *What if I'm not just grateful to be free? What if I'm deeply angry and sad that I don't have a mom?* Who had a full, rich life, but one where the abuse memories were never faint.

It would have meant a lot to me if, instead of focusing on the goal of normalizing myself, my therapists had used more tools to honor dissociation, self-injury, and stimming as survival skills, not marks of how scarred I still was. If they could have talked about what changes we needed to make in our communities so that there were many examples of crazy femmes not having to hide our crazy to be loved and, more than that, respected and valued as leaders. What if I'd seen femme leaders who weren't loved just when we were infallible but also when we were curled up on the floor having a panic attack? What if there were revolutionary and generous work structures that allowed us to call in crazy or sad, to cry at our desks and never be seen as unreliable when we did so? I wonder how it would have landed if a therapist had refrained from saying I'd "never be done" and instead shown me pictures of what that could look like.

Of course, that would mean moving from an individual survivor support model to one where survivors and our madness and our survivorhood were truly loved and honored. Where communities had mad and trauma-surviving folks as leaders—and not just ones who were super really good at never showing their crazy. Some of our communities have that. Many don't.

AS A DISABLED person, my experience of my disability changed 1,000 percent when I learned from disabled friends that instead of seeing my disabled body as broken and wrong and shameful, I could see myself as part of a lineage of disabled genius friends, warriors, and lovers. Instead of being marginalized from inaccessible community, forever on the edge or unable to get in or stay at the queer club, I could have a deeply satisfying crip family and community. I could organize and communicate my art on Skype, in my living room, in the accessible spaces on the database we collectively created.

And I wonder: How would my experience of my survivorhood change if it, following a disability justice precept, moved from being seen as an individual, sad, and shameful experience to a common, normal, and collective one that I had every right to access and create movements for, with work and art in mind? If I could see others who were leaders, lovers, and cherished community members whose breakdowns and triggers were an openly loved part of who they were? Would this be survivor collective access?

THERE ARE STILL not enough of these long-term survivor stories, so I am going to offer mine. I'm forty-two. I live in a house with my amazing femme of color partner and friends, plus two cats, in a greenbelt strip in Southside Seattle where there are big trees and blackberry bushes and a secret creek that is also ten minutes from Wendy's. The survivor, working class femme of color love I get from my partner has transformed my heart and my cunt and my life. Living together is amazing, and also was super hard in ways I in no way expected. Moving in hit me with all the PTSD from past abuse in the world.

I love my friends and I have panic attacks that lay me out for two days. I'm still unpacking deep shame I have around "being crazy" and around being the survivor of childhood sexual abuse that is stigmatized (mother-daughter, happened early). By *unpacking* I mean sometimes it hits like a gut punch in the middle of my day, in the middle of negotiating sex or teaching a workshop. Grief about not having a mom brought me to my knees, and I stayed there for a long time, and I cancelled shit and worked in pajamas and cried longer than I thought there were days. I didn't know that grief was there. I can be defensive and stubborn as hell. I can snap and get into a fight over who gets to use a cutting board. I can be wrong. I can have a meltdown. I can be frozen. I can jerk off for hours and not be able to get out of bed. I can win awards. I can make dinner for friends.

I have somatic flashbacks of my rape. Still. I'm still scared to talk to my family, and visiting my home state or driving through my hometown is never something I do casually, never without an escape plan and much preparation. I experience months of joy and weeks that get sucked under when I trip over a wire and a trap door opens.

I am not normal, at all, and I have not forgotten anything. Nor do I want to. I do not want an individualized healing. I want to enjoy the shit out of my life, and I want to use the knowledge I have gained from surviving rape to transform the world with others who share my pain.

I do not want to be fixed if being fixed means being bleached of memory, untaught by what I have learned through this miracle of surviving. My survivorhood is not an individual problem. I want the communion of all of us who have survived, and the knowledge.

I do not want to be fixed. I want to change the world. I want to be alive, awake, grieving, and full of joy. And I am.

Notes

1. For a Black, Indigenous, and brown feminist analysis of the non-profit industrial complex, see *The Revolution Will Not Be Funded*, INCITE Women of Color Against Violence (Durham, NC: Duke University Press, 2017).

2. For a much more detailed account of a disabled queer survivor grappling with cure and its complexities, check out Eli Clare's *Brilliant Imperfection* (Durham, NC: Duke University Press, 2017).

3. Collective access is a term describing the ways sick and disabled people can and do create interdependent access for each other. Collective access is in opposition to many of the ways access is commonly understood and practiced, which is as charities with much gatekeeping and little autonomy, administered by able-bodied people who treat disabled people as passive recipients. Collective access emphasizes the ways disabled people can and do care for each other, and the power, knowledge, and labor we have done and still do. For more about collective access, check out creatingcollectiveaccess.wordpress.com.

4. Disability justice is an intersectional movement for liberation centering the lives and leadership of disabled queer and trans people and disabled Black and brown people (and those of us who are both). Invented in 2005 by Patty Berne, Leroy Moore, Mia Mingus, Eli Clare, and Sebastian Margaret, disability justice both builds on earlier disability rights organizing and critiques its whiteness and single issue focus on independence and gaining legal rights, and argues for interdependence, mutual aid, and dismantling capitalism and colonialism. For more, check out sinsinvalid.org or *Skin, Tooth, and Bone: The Basis of Movement Is Our People: A Disability Justice Primer.*

THE MOTHER
YOU NEED

•

Elisabeth de Mariaffi

●

I WAS TWENTY-SEVEN YEARS old by the time I met her. I was, at that age, a mother of two, a homeowner— a mortgage-holder. This is important. I'd spent my early twenties tangling myself up with all the markers of adulthood. Adults are sovereign and powerful. If you have children yourself, you are safe from the powerlessness of childhood. Aren't you?

Ingrid was my doctor's wife, a pretty woman maybe twenty years older than me with a New Zealand accent, both foreign and immediately intimate. She was old enough to be my mother, but barely. That part is important, too, I think. That part is the point.

I WAS AT the doctor's office. I can't now remember the context exactly, though I doubt this was an appointment I made with myself in mind, but rather one of those endless family doc visits you find yourself on when you have small children. Small children are forever getting sick. I know that I was exhausted, something he could surely see.

I would not have chosen a male doctor, but we were living in a town about an hour outside of Toronto. Family doctors were scarce. We were lucky to have him, but luckier still to have found someone so kind. So when he asked me how I was—*But, really, how are* you?—I told him.

I think something's wrong, I said.

My daughter, my eldest, had just begun nursery school, a lovely cooperative school with tiny classes and an experienced teacher and only the most generous-hearted parent volunteers. My daughter loved the school. But I could not stop crying.

I could not shake the idea of what might happen to her, small and alone in the world, and a girl. Two mornings a week I left her there and walked away, her baby brother strapped to my chest. I was not afraid of the teacher, or an accident, or even of her loneliness. I was afraid of the fathers.

The fathers: men who might stay and volunteer for the morning. I was sure I could not trust them. At night, I stood in my kitchen, trembling in my wrists. I had become convinced this meant I wanted to slice them through.

Postpartum depression, I told my doctor. *It is, isn't it?*

The anxiety was so bad, at times, I felt I could barely stay upright.

This is not really what postpartum looks like, he said. (You remember I said he was kind.) There was a pause. Then: *Did anything happen in your childhood? My wife is a therapist. I think she's very good.*

This may seem unconventional, but remember, we lived in a town, not a city. The same doctor gave me his own daughter's hand-me-downs for my little girl.

Did anything happen in your childhood?

I told him it was pretty normal. Middle class. Only child. Apart from this thing where my best friend was raped and killed when we were nine.

This essay is not about that.

EXCEPT, OF COURSE, it is.

This essay is not about one terrible assault, and how I fought my way through the aftermath. I want to say up front that I know many other women have been through traumas greater than I.

(As I write this, I am aware of how cheap and terrible it is to have to play the brutal game of Hierarchy-of-Abuses, a game that is forced upon women by the same authority that demands of us a flawless victimhood, without which we risk condemnation as liars or drama queens. First, there is the question of whether this authority will believe our assault happened in the first place; next, whether it was horrific enough to warrant concern.)

What I want to talk about is the death by a thousand cuts of many small assaults, how they fold over onto each other, and how I (mostly) shook out the pleats, managed to (mostly) lay them flat. There were many smaller assaults, a lifetime of assaults, really: this experience makes me similar to every woman you know. And I got through not by myself, but because someone helped me.

DESPITE MY BEING a writer by trade, I've never believed in writing my way through it. Or I don't believe that I can. (I know this works for other people.) I learned over time to tell my stories in casual conversation by paring them down to the essentials, diminishing them, sometimes going for the laugh, separating them from me and my very real body, my body that actually is me. That kind of storytelling operates as a device—something to keep connection at bay. The hardest writing work I've done has attempted to translate the worst moments of my own story into a story that can be read, by someone else. Something meant, in fact, to breed connection.

I have to do the work first, and even then, I struggle through. I'm struggling now. Write a scene. Begin with a scene.

This game, Hierarchy-of-Abuses, is where we began, when I first started seeing Ingrid. I told her that the thing I feared was postpartum depression—PPD was getting a lot of press at that time. What she wanted me to talk about was my friend's murder.

I couldn't wrap my head around the idea that someone else's death could be a trauma that affected me. It was my friend, after all, and not me who was left alone in a playground during the coldest month of the year; she who had welcomed the conversation with a grown man, who had agreed to follow him back to his rooming house; her screams, not mine, the neighbors had overheard. Her body that was folded into a freezer and left behind.

As a child, I was a precocious reader. I told Ingrid I'd followed the case minutely, reading the details about the search as they were laid out in the *Toronto Star*: the door-to-door, the witness statements, the dogs let loose in the city's ravines. And later, the discovery of my friend's body.

How did you get your hands on the paper? Ingrid asked. *Where were your parents?* This was not a question that had occurred to me before.

You were a good reader, my mother said. *We couldn't stop you.*

I think it more likely, now, that my parents were themselves poorly equipped to deal with the reality that had been thrust upon them. Immigrant families run small, and ours was no exception. With extended family almost all overseas, there was no wealth of aunts and uncles and cousins to share the burden. It must seem grossly unfair to escape war and build a home in a new, promising country, only to have trauma follow you there.

Anyway, an only child is always a de facto small adult in the family. So what if I wanted to know every detail? Maybe reading the papers every day gave me a feeling of control.

The facts of what had happened to my friend built up in my own body, sharp-sided and expanding. I closed off, sealing myself in with it. I had a safe male teacher, a good and decent father, two jovial godfathers who often came around. I don't remember feeling uncomfortable around men before the age of nine, but the change, when it came, was stark and immediate.

TWO YEARS AFTER my friend's murder: I'm playing in a public swimming pool when a man swims by, slides his hand inside my bathing suit, and tries to penetrate me with a finger.

I would like to say I spun around, yelled out, held his head underwater. I did not. I froze. I know that he was under the water; I know that he swam away. I never saw his face, and it happened so quickly I couldn't have identified him, anyway. You have to be operating in a state of vigilance to mark identifying details in a moment like that; most eleven-year-old girls have not learned that vigilance yet. This is why they are such common targets.

My mother was not far away when this happened. I got out of the pool, pulled her aside, and did what eleven-year-old girls are supposed to do: I told. I remember that I was crying.

Oh, she said. *That's just a thing men do.*

She sent me back in.

I'M WRITING THIS during a time that feels both galvanizing and exhausting. It's been a rough year for women. After months of #MeToo, a mass public disclosure of sexual harassment and assault, there's something restorative in being asked to talk about healing. Therapy is a long road and, at times, an indentured one: you've got to get in to get out. It wasn't the first way I got through, but it was Ingrid who helped me to finally put my own puzzle together. By that time, there were a lot of pieces. Part of this is because trauma breeds trauma, maybe, or makes you more vulnerable to it. You are taught to fear, and your look of fearfulness marks you.

Where were we? Ah: here I am, poolside, sliding back into the shallow end. Drowning a little. I've relived the moment a million times through my daughter's childhood. There's a difficult piece here that is about a woman in my own family who did not stand up for me. How is it possible that she did not? Speaking now as an adult and as a mother, it is unfathomable to me that my own mother did nothing that day. I felt I had been dropped from a great height.

After the incident at the pool, I closed off a little more. Other, similar, incidents came around and found me. (You are taught to fear, and your look of fearfulness marks you.) By the time I was fifteen, I had learned to keep my body firmly in my own control by starving it. At 97 pounds, I was admitted to hospital, something that could, I guess, have also been traumatic but in fact gave me a month of breathing space. Time out. At 102 pounds, they let me out again. I had by that time decided that anorexia was not the form I wanted to occupy in the world, and I learned to eat by applying the same discipline I'd used to starve myself: the steel-eyed resolve of an athlete.

The guidance counselor who'd come to bring me my homework twice a week was also, by chance, the high school cross-country coach. At 115 pounds, I took up running. Every footfall brought me again to earth, the same earth, every time. I learned to make time on the downhills by stretching long and allowing gravity to pull me. I leaped downhill. Falling did not scare me. Running taught me not to fear it—not to fear being dropped from a great height. The earth rose up to meet me, consistent and reliable and hard-packed. I ran the city finals. I was nominated MVP. A decidedly better way to get through.

A year later, I was eating dinner with my mother in a foreign country. The restaurant owner, a man in his late forties, came around to our table maybe a bit too often; my mother commented that he seemed to like me. Later, he followed me into the bathroom, pushed my face against the wall, and took his cock out. The rough feel of his hand in my pants.

This is a near-miss story. I can't remember what I did to talk my way out of there, without yelling, without making a scene, my cheek against the tile. I was clever and calm and brash. I was drowning, a little.

I came back to the table, finished my dinner, and said nothing. I knew, by sixteen, not to bother. This was just another man. Just a thing men do. I'd learned to manage it.

GLORIA STEINEM SAYS some very smart and empathetic things about mothers. We "spend a lot of time denying our mothers," she says, speaking to *Interview* back in 1984. "We understand other women earlier than we understand our mothers because we're trying so hard to say, 'I'm not going to be like my mother' that we blame her for her condition. If we didn't blame her for her condition, we would have to admit that it could happen to us, too... Even if they raped us, we will blame our mothers for not protecting us instead of blaming [the men] who actually did it."

I mean, that's true, isn't it? The villain here is the man who killed my friend, or the man in the swimming pool, or the man in the restaurant. I am quite sure my mother did not mean to abandon me. I do think it's possible that she didn't see any other options. Some of this has to do with her own fear, or else self-preservation. She had grown up with a wildly abusive father, slept two years in a refugee camp, another two in rooming houses as a new immigrant. At fourteen, she stepped between her parents, defying her father, and saved her own mother's life. Maybe, by the time I came of age, there was no saving left in her.

I can get that. Denial is not a complicated story. The reason for disbelieving, or diminishing, is simple: we don't want these stories to be true. We don't want it to be true when it's our friend who has assaulted a woman; we don't want nice-looking varsity swimming stars to also be back-alley rapists; we don't want it to be true that enough men regularly and casually assault girls to make it unsafe to take your eleven-year-old to a public pool on a hot Toronto after-noon. If it is true, then it is terrible. In this way, I can see diminishment as a kind of defense mechanism. But diminishing, or disbelieving, in this defensive way only reduces women to casualties in someone else's story—the story that's about men, not women; the story that's about accu-sation, instead of about harm.

I am aware that I am leaning hard on mothers here—why does no one ever ask, *Where was the father?*—but the reality is that when you've been assaulted by a man, that experience changes your relationship to all men. This real-ity makes me sad, but my sadness does not make it any less so. We need to depend on women listening, because it's probably only women we will feel safe enough to disclose to.

Our mothers' absences don't lessen our need to fill those spaces. I am not writing this to indict my mother, or to drop her, in turn, from a great height—though, let's face it, I may not tell her about this essay. (What would it serve?) I'm writing this because I think we all have to find the mothers we need, at different times in our lives. I think it's okay to go looking.

IT'S NO COINCIDENCE that the moment I needed saving the most was the moment my own daughter was just old enough to begin navigating the world without me, off at nursery school on her own. I see now that the anxiety I was up against was not only the old boogeyman fear—*What if something happens to her?*—but also something more piercingly intimate: *What if I fail to protect her?*

As a girl and a young woman, my focus had been on getting through by getting control over my own body—in ways that were healthy, or not. But now, with the loveliest three-year-old girl in my charge, I had a new assignment. I wanted her to be safe. I also wanted her to be fearless. This seemed an uphill task in a moment when I felt crushed by anxiety myself. In order to teach her how to not be afraid, I had to model it. But to model it, I needed some mothering of my own.

There were things that men did that almost derailed me entirely. What got me through was a woman.

THE SORT OF therapy Ingrid practices is called bioenergetics. If this sounds to you like the kind of thing that requires crystals and/or caftan-wearing, then you are not alone. I'm a practical-minded daughter of immigrants. No one in my family had *gone to therapy*. In my family, we *suffered through*.

In fact, the premise behind bioenergetics is simple: psychological trauma moves into the body. You can use your body to work it out. As someone who had been using her body to work it out, one way or another, all the way along, the practice made sense to me. We began most sessions with a grounding exercise—not unlike yoga's mountain pose—and some deep, loud sighs.

The purpose of grounding is connection: to the moment, to yourself, but most importantly, to the ground beneath your feet. When I first started running, I loved the feel of the ground rising up to meet me. Good ol' earth, steady and reliable. *Feel your feet*, Ingrid said, which sounds silly out of context, but anxiety can feel like falling—like you might fall forever. Feeling the solid ground at your feet is a pretty good remedy for that.

There were some other techniques on offer—things you might more easily associate with therapy—a kind of primal screaming, and that thing where you tap your wrists and temples. But what actually grounded me was the more important reliability: knowing that every week, Ingrid would be there. There's no therapeutic fast track. It's about time, and it's about willingness, and work. For me, it was equally about the shepherd. Sometimes we just need someone to listen and look after us. Ingrid was that woman for me. What I remember most is the mother-care.

Some of this mother-care was a bit tough: I wanted an easy answer. For a long time, I insisted that the problem had to be related to those post-baby hormones. I liked the idea because it was the sort of problem that, if you wait long enough, might simply go away. Hormones eventually regulate. Ingrid shook her head, equally insistent: I had a kind of posttraumatic stress.

Some of the mother-care was about acceptance. A thing I learned: you can tell a story over and over, in truncated and practiced ways, and use that practice to separate yourself from it. Maybe this is more true of writers than other people, or maybe, as I said earlier, it's just me. This is where I figured out that I'd been using my way of relating my own stories—anecdotally, throwaway—as a distancing technique. The opposite of writing-as-therapy. I'd been steadily fictionalizing them.

Therapy is mostly a slow burn, but if you want to hear about a breakthrough moment, for me it was the day I realized I'd been telling these stories, both my friend's murder and whatever had happened to me, for years, as though I was reporting the news or, sometimes, glibly repeating some satirical internet fare. Ingrid said something like: *This is* your *story.* The realization hit me like a wave.

Wait, I said. *This really happened. To me. I was that kid.*

For the first time, I had, as the storyteller, empathy for the girl in the story while comprehending that that girl was also me. It sounds simplistic, but this was a radical shift in my thinking. A bright, painful moment.

The bottom dropped out. I went outside and it was snowing, and I sat in my car and cried. The radio was playing Weezer's "Island in the Sun," a song I still think of as profoundly sad, a song that for me is about loss. Things got harder then, for a long time, but it was the beginning of things getting better.

THERAPY IS A tricky thing. It's mostly about finding a therapist who is really listening. I don't mean just listening as you sit in a soft chair and tell that old story, but really listening, listening for what's underneath. Someone who will pick out clues and use them, strike the fine balance between comfort and discomfort, lead you back through the most difficult moments in your life and out the other side.

What I needed was the right someone to say the right things at the right time, and so many of those things seem banal in this context. *It's okay, it's all right.* But when we say, *It's okay*, we accept that things have *not* been okay. That acknowledgment washed over me like relief, like a soft hand at my brow.

Or maybe it was the right someone to teach me to say the right things to myself: *This is just my anxiety.* When you're living with anxiety, one of the worst worries is that you will start worrying. In a moment of relative calm, my sharpest fear would kick in—the fear that I would start feeling afraid again. If that sounds like a crazy-making cycle, you're right. It is. Cutting it off at the pass worked for me. *It's okay. This is just my anxiety.*

This basic loving-kindness, in combination with a steadfast validation of my own experience, is, I guess, what I mean by mother-care. If that seems overly simple, it's because most of the work of therapy is done by the survivor, and it's lonely and it's arduous and it takes years. So, yeah, you need someone lovely to hold your hand through that.

Before we parted ways, Ingrid asked me the most important question of my life, a question that hung briefly in the air before catapulting me out of an abusive relationship and into my life as I know it now. The details of that marriage and that question are surely a topic for an essay of their own, but she was able to ask it because she had spent, at that point, years listening to me. Listening not just to what I said, but truly listening to who I was.

A FEW YEARS later, I moved away from Ontario, and this gave me the freedom to write about the Toronto that made me afraid. The resulting novel, *The Devil You Know*, is in its loosest terms a story about women and fear. It felt, in the writing, very much to me like a book that was equal parts a love letter to home and a portrayal of the scariest time in my life.

In 1993, the arrest of Paul Bernardo—the highest-profile serial killer and serial rapist in Toronto history—brought ten years of citywide panic to an end. Boogeyman, indeed. The papers had named Bernardo the Scarborough Rapist; those attacks were the news of the day when I was coming of age. The media furor through those years, and the accompanying message—that to be a woman is to be a victim, that to be female is to be afraid—formed the historical and emotional backdrop of my novel.

Writing this book was not therapy. Writing this book was something I could not have done without the years of therapy that had gone before. Without the work, without my therapist's guiding hand, I don't even know if I could have written it at all; certainly, I would have been writing from a place of fear, rather than trying to create a place of connection.

I still carry Ingrid's voice along with me—she had that lilting accent, so I always know when the voice is hers—and it's this voice that I've relied on to get me through mothering my own children, especially my daughter. Her words that I use when my kids need help, and when friends come to me, and when strangers come—and they did come, taking me by surprise, after *Devil* was published.

In the wake of the book's release, I was prepared to answer intimate questions about the murder of my friend. What I didn't see coming were the letters from readers: other women looking for that same listening ear and gentleness I had found in Ingrid, women looking to disclose their own sexual assaults and their fear to someone who would listen. I tried to follow the model that had been laid out for me. Listening, a genuine response. It was unexpected.

If we're trained to deny our own experience, it is much easier to then deny the experience of someone else. It is easier to diminish than to listen, because these stories encroach on our own lives. If it is true, then it is terrible. It means we must all live in fear. It makes fear our only birthright. This is why the public rhetoric around believing women is more than just politics. What I learned from Ingrid was the value of caring mentorship. A hand extended. We all have to find the mothers we need.

I keep my own goal clear: be a safe woman for other women to talk to. I am no therapist. I often worry that I am not able to do enough. But I can at least reach out and take your hand. I can refuse to send you back in.

I LIVE BY the ocean now. It's not a calm place: the Atlantic is not something you live companionably alongside. My mother moved to be close to me; at the same moment, my daughter moved away to begin her own adventure. I still run long distance. It's rocky here, but there's something extra grounding about that, weather and a landscape that require my attention.

Ingrid is long-lost to me now. In theory, I do not need her anymore. We all leave our mothers. I am both grateful and heartbroken, it seems.

CONTRIBUTORS

Amber Dawn is a writer and creative facilitator living on unceded Coast Salish Territories (Vancouver, Canada). She is the author of four books and the editor of two anthologies, all of which explore the confluence of queer and survivor identities.

Gwen Benaway is a trans girl of Anishinaabe and Métis descent. She has published three collections of poetry, *Ceremonies for the Dead*, *Passage*, and *Holy Wild*. Her fourth collection of poetry, *Aperture*, is forthcoming from Book*hug in spring 2020.

Elly Danica is a semiretired warrior woman, writer, and fiber artist.

Elisabeth de Mariaffi is the Giller-nominated author of one book of short stories and two novels. She lives by the ocean, in St. John's, Newfoundland.

Alicia Elliott is an award-winning Tuscarora writer from Six Nations of the Grand River Territory living in Brantford, Ontario. She's the author of the book of essays *A Mind Spread Out on the Ground*.

Karyn L. Freedman is an associate professor of philosophy at the University of Guelph. Her book, *One Hour in Paris: A True Story of Rape and Recovery*, won the BC National Award for Canadian Non-Fiction.

Lauren McKeon is the digital editor at the Walrus. Her first book, *F-Bomb: Dispatches from the War on Feminism*, was published in 2017 and shortlisted for the Kobo Emerging Writer Prize.

Juliane Okot Bitek is a poet. She lives in the unceded, ancestral, and traditional lands of the Squamish, Musqueam, and Tsleil-Waututh peoples, in Vancouver.

Heather O'Neill is the author of *Lullabies for Little Criminals*, *The Girl Who Was Saturday Night*, *Daydreams of Angels*, and *The Lonely Hearts Hotel*. Her work has been shortlisted for the Orange Prize, the Governor General's Award, and the Giller Prize in two consecutive years. She has been awarded the Hugh MacLennan Prize and the Danuta Gleed Award, and has won the CBC Canada Reads competition.

Soraya Palmer hails from Brooklyn, NYC, with roots in Trinidad and Jamaica. Her prose has been published in *Hazlitt*, *Ploughshares*, *Callaloo*, *Black Warrior Review*, *Ninth Letter*, and elsewhere. She is at work on a novel and a book of essays.

Leah Lakshmi Piepzna-Samarasinha is the author of *Care Work: Dreaming Disability Justice*; *Dirty River: A Queer Femme of Color Dreaming Her Way Home* (shortlisted for the Lambda and Publishing Triangle Awards, ALA Above the Rainbow List); *Bodymap* (shortlisted for the Publishing Triangle Award); *Love Cake* (Lambda Literary Award winner); and *Consensual Genocide*, and is coeditor of *The Revolution Starts at Home: Confronting Intimate Violence in Activist Communities*. A lead artist with Sins Invalid, her writing has been widely published, with recent work in PBS Newshour, Poets.org's Poetry and the Body folio, *The Deaf Poets Society, Bitch, Self, TruthOut*, and *The Body Is Not an Apology*.

Kai Cheng Thom is a writer, performer, and community worker in Toronto, traditional Indigenous territory. A two-time Lambda Literary Award finalist, and the winner of the 2017 Dayne Ogilvie Prize for LGBTQ Emerging Writers, she is the author of a novel, a poetry collection, and a children's book.